MEAT &
POTATOES
CATHOLICISM

MEAT & POTATOES CATHOLICISM

REV. JOSEPH F. CLASSEN

Our Sunday Visitor Publishing Division
Our Sunday Visitor, Inc.
Huntington, Indiana 46750

CONTENTS

Struggling with theological education. Why so
many Catholics don't know their faith. Getting
back to the "meat and potatoes" of our faith. The
purpose of this book.

Addressing the reasons people quit the Church.
We must stay! What is the Church? The Church
is our home.

God's signs. God in Scripture — *something*
happened! Manifestation of the Divine outside of
Scripture. God in the sacraments.

The transforming power of water and the
sacrament of Baptism. The Rite of Baptism. Our
baptismal vocation. The commitment,
responsibility, and journey of Baptism.

ACKNOWLEDGMENTS

THIS BOOK IS DEDICATED to all those who bravely preach and teach the *meat and potatoes* of the Catholic faith in our dioceses, parishes, schools, and on the home front. May the Lord continue to nourish you and give you strength, courage, and an abundance of his grace. I'd like to also offer a special word of thanks to Archbishop Raymond Burke for his support and willingness to be a part of this project.

God bless you!
Fr. Joseph Classen

FOREWORD

IN HIS OWN EXPERIENCE of growing up in the Catholic faith and in his pastoral care of the faithful since his ordination to the priesthood on May 24, 2003, Fr. Joseph Classen has witnessed a great hunger for our Lord Jesus Christ and for the saving truths that Christ communicates to us in the Church. Fr. Classen has seen directly how an insubstantial, even if well-intentioned, presentation of the Catholic faith leaves the faithful dangerously adrift in a world sorely beset with the evils of materialism, secularism and relativism.

Without a firm grounding in the faith and its practice, today's Catholic is easily led to compromise his or her relationship with Christ and his Church for the sake of practicing a false tolerance and a "political correctness" that promises to make Catholicism acceptable to everyone. The danger of compromising the Catholic faith in our culture is not just theoretical. It has been sadly realized in the widespread phenomenon of "cafeteria Catholicism."

At the same time, the failure to give a direct and sound account of the faith leaves those who are not Catholic in confusion with regard to what Catholics believe and practice. This danger is also not merely theoretical. Not infrequently, middle-aged and young adult Catholics comment to me that they are not able or are not confident to hand on the faith to others, including their children, because the catechesis that they received was inadequate and even false. The new evangelization of our world depends upon the solid and strong witness of all Catholics in all of the arenas of human activity and endeavor in which they find themselves. Without such witness, Catholics not only do not provide for others the light which they are seeking, but they themselves end up lost in the darkness of our totally secularized society.

What should Catholics and others interested in the Catholic faith do in the face of the pervasive confusion and error regarding the Catholic faith, even among Catholics? It is certainly not helpful to become mired in discouragement over the situation of a certain Catholic illiteracy or in the assignment of blame to those who, over the past several decades, have failed to provide a more adequate catechesis. There is really only one correct response — the response that the Servant of God Pope John Paul II and Pope Paul VI before him constantly urged. It is the new evangelization, that is, the teaching, the celebrating, and the living of our Catholic faith with the enthusiasm and energy of the first disciples of our Lord and of the missionaries who brought the Catholic faith to our land. It is embracing our Catholic faith, in all of its richness, as if for the first time.

In his Post-synodal Apostolic Exhortation *Christifideles laici* "On the Vocation and Mission of the Lay Faithful in the Church and in the World," the Servant of God Pope John Paul II described the challenge of the faithful today, which is "a result of a constant spreading of an indifference to religion, of secularism and atheism" and which "inspires and sustains a life lived 'as if God did not exist.'" He declared: "This indifference to religion and the practice of religion devoid of true meaning in the face of life's very serious problems, are not less worrying and upsetting when compared with declared atheism" (No. 34).

What response does Pope John Paul II urge? He reminds us of Christ's own mandate to all in the Church, in every state of life:

Certainly the command of Jesus: "Go and preach the Gospel" always maintains its vital value and its ever-pressing obligation. Nevertheless, the *present situation*, not only of the world but also of many parts of the Church, *absolutely demands that the word of Christ receive a more ready and generous obedience*. Every disciple is personally called by name; no disciple can withhold making a response: "Woe to me, if I do not preach the Gospel" (1 Cor 9:16) (No. 33).

Before the present and urgent call to give a solid and strong witness of obedience to the faith, it is the task of all in the Church to know the faith, to celebrate the faith, and to practice the faith in everyday life. All in the Church are called to be about the work of preaching the Gospel. It is imperative, therefore, to deepen our knowledge of the Catholic faith, especially in the context of the questioning and confusion about the fundamental truths of the faith, both within the Church and in society in general.

Knowing his own experience of confusion about the faith and its practice, and seeing how those whom he serves as a priest suffer from a widespread confusion and error regarding the Catholic faith, Fr. Classen has prepared the first volume of his *Meat & Potatoes Catholicism*, a response of pastoral charity in the face of the hunger for the truth and love of Christ on the part of many. The response is a plain-spoken and substantial presentation of the teaching of the Church. *Meat & Potatoes Catholicism* provides a practical and reliable guide to those who want to deepen their knowledge of the faith for the sake of living more fully in Christ and of drawing others to life in Christ. It is a most worthy tool of the new evangelization that is so very much needed in our time.

Meat & Potatoes Catholicism provides the substance of the Church's teaching. At the same time, Fr. Classen gives timely indications of the sources by which the reader can further deepen his knowledge of the truths of the faith. The primary source is, of course, the *Catechism of the Catholic Church*, which not only enunciates the content of our faith and its practice but also leads us to the Holy Scriptures and Sacred Tradition, to the *Code of Canon Law*, and to the secure teachers of the faith down the Christian centuries. In his customary direct manner, Fr. Classen also indicates that he frequently relies upon the writings of the Servant of God Archbishop Fulton J. Sheen in his presentation of the faith.

Most fittingly, in the first volume of *Meat & Potatoes Catholicism*, Fr. Classen draws upon his personal and pastoral experience to present the Church's teaching on the Sacraments. The Sacraments, above all, the Holy Eucharist, are the source of our life in Christ in the Church and, at the same time, the highest expression of Christ's life within us. Regarding the Holy Eucharist, Pope Benedict XVI succinctly observed:

> In this sacrament, the Lord truly becomes food for us, to satisfy our hunger for truth and freedom. Since only the truth can make us free (cf. Jn 8:32), Christ becomes for us the food of truth. (Pope Benedict XVI, Post-synodal Apostolic Exhortation *Sacramentum caritatis*, "On the Eucharist as the Source and Summit of the Church's Life and Mission," Feb. 22, 2007, n. 2)

The most fitting and effective way to help Catholics to deepen their understanding of the faith and to attract others to the Catholic Church is the presentation of the Church's teaching on the sacraments. Fr. Classen presents each of the sacraments with care, placing his presentation within the context of today's frequently-asked questions and common areas of confusion about the sacraments.

May this first volume of *Meat & Potatoes Catholicism* provide for you the solid nourishment of the presentation of the Catholic faith in its integrity. May it be a source of inspiration and strength for you in taking up the work of the new evangelization.

I conclude by expressing the hope that Fr. Joseph Classen will be able to continue his work of pastoral charity, begun with this volume, by writing additional volumes of *Meat & Potatoes Catholicism*.

The Most Reverend Raymond Leo Burke
Archbishop of St. Louis
December 3, 2007 — Memorial of
St. Francis Xavier, Priest

INTRODUCTION

THE MALNOURISHED CATHOLIC

ON A PARTICULARLY PLEASANT autumn afternoon in 2006, a Saturday afternoon as I recall, I found myself at one of my first book signings. I pleasantly greeted folks, visited with old familiar friends, talked shop with the more inquisitive customers, and tried my best to sign my name and write out their requested personalized messages in a manner that would not resemble the proverbial "chicken scratch" that my third grade teacher dubbed my penmanship as being.

At one point during the afternoon, an older lady slowly approached the table where I was set up and picked up a book, gently thumbed through it, and then from behind her sagging reading glasses, gave me a rather abhorred look and inquired with a tone of distain, "Now is this a book that normal people can read? All you priests and bishops write these books that the rest of us can't understand. And let me tell you, we're not impressed! We don't have degrees in theology! Most of the things you guys write don't make a lick of sense to us who sit in the pew. You're just out to impress and outdo each other with all your fancy words. When are you going to start writing things for us?" I was a bit taken back for a moment by her candor, but actually I was glad to hear her brutally honest comment, because that's exactly how I felt about so much of the catechetical (educational) material that has come out over the years.

STRUGGLING WITH THEOLOGICAL EDUCATION

LATER THAT DAY, as I reflected more deeply on this lady's comments, I began to have flashbacks of my own religious education and the frustration I experienced, especially during my days in the seminary... (imagine dreamy theatrical flashback sounds)... ah yes, there I was, the first day of Latin I... "Good morning, class. Open your books to page one. Read please. *'Per sapientiam enim Dei manifestantur divinorum abscondita, producuntur creaturarum opera, nec tantum producuntur...* (and so on).' Okay, for your homework, translate that along with everything else in Chapter 1. See you on Wednesday. Class dismissed." And with that, my jaw dropped and my head began to pound in frustrated disbelief as my seminary theological education had begun.

"Oh Lord, what have I gotten myself into?" I asked as I sat in my tiny, cell-sized room that evening. Gazing in agony at the stacks of books on my desk seemed like standing at the base of Mt. Everest with no idea how to properly climb. I was utterly overwhelmed. For a guy who disliked school from the first day of kindergarten, the idea of spending the better part of the next decade studying theology and philosophy was too much to fathom, much less bear at the moment. I hesitantly pulled a book off the mountainous stack and pondered its contents. After attempting to make sense of the first few paragraphs, I realized that it might as well have been written in Chinese. It seemed hopeless.

As the semester rolled on and my grades continued to ride the tide of mediocrity and occasionally plummet from the undertow, I knew there was no easy way out of this one. I couldn't take classes like "Folk Guitar" or "Ultimate Frisbee" to easily boost my pummeled GPA. There was no escape. There was no hanging out at local college bars to drown my sorrows in cheap, watery beer and laugh away my academic demise, hoping to somehow once again miraculously pull things together at the last moment, as I often had a knack for doing in the past. This was serious business. I was, in a sense, a professional student. It was my job to study. I had to either step up, or step off.

With my synaptic connections (fueled by pots of coffee) firing rapidly on all cylinders like a well-tuned engine, I kept force-feeding my brain the foreign, mysterious information that I was being exposed to day after day. "How can it be this difficult to learn about Christ and the Church?" I kept asking myself. "How can becoming a priest possibly be so hard? What does any of this stuff have to do with the faith? How will any of this make me a holier man? Isn't the gospel message supposed to be simple to understand (though challenging to live)? Shouldn't a child be able to understand the teachings of Christ and be able to implement them in his or her life? How in the world is all this stuff going to be of any help to the good, hardworking folks who sit in the pews on Sunday morning?" The questions just kept coming as I grew more and more frustrated with the constant intellectual gymnastics.

In those first few agonizing semesters, I realized that I was, in fact, truly learning the Catholic faith for the first time, albeit in an extremely detailed, in-depth manner. I was "cutting my teeth" as they say, to be able to acquire the cognitive tools and mental discipline to explore the deepest recesses of faith and Sacred Tradition. I would often spend the first part of my study sessions just translating the material into layman's terms. As time went on, I came to the conclusion that up until that point, my Catholic education was on par with a fifth grader.

Although I had taken it upon myself to attempt to relearn the essentials of my faith before entering the seminary, I realized that I didn't even scratch the surface; I didn't even know what the surface was comprised of, for that matter. I also realized that the vast majority of Catholics of my generation, and many in the generation before and after, were probably at about the same level of understanding that I was, even though many of us received a "Catholic education" in both grade school and high school.

I began to interrogate myself further as to the disappearance of my religious databank: "Did I just not pay attention in school, especially religion class? Did I just forget everything I learned over the years? Had all that knowledge simply disintegrated from too many of those cheap, watery beers in college?" Then the most poignant question of all hit me: "Did I ever really even learn the basics of my faith?" As I pondered that final question, I began having more flashbacks about the nature of my religious education and that of those around my same era, give or take ten years.

WHY SO MANY CATHOLICS DON'T KNOW THEIR FAITH

THOSE OF US WHO RECEIVED a Catholic education during the late '60s, through the '70s and into the early '80s were subjected not only to a time of tumultuous social change, but we also experienced significant changes in our Church that came about from the Second Vatican Council. There is still great debate today over the positive and negative effects of Vatican II, as well as the challenges that came in implementing its teachings. Some feel that this council is the greatest thing that ever happened to the Catholic Church, whereas others feel it was the beginning of the end.

On the parish level, there were those who joyfully embraced the changes in the Mass and the fresh approach to things that Vatican II ushered in, and there were those who defiantly held on to the way things were and did not want to budge an inch. The result for students of this time was that we were subjected to opposite extremes of religious education. There was a great deal of catechetical ideological clashing that went on.

While the vast majority of our Catholic teachers (nuns, brother, priests and laity) were wonderful, heroic, dedicated, truly inspirational souls, there were more than a few yardstick-wielding instructors whose approach to teaching the faith was, "Learn about Jesus or die!" Then there was the opposite extreme: attempting to learn the faith from teachers who were ex-hippies (no offense, ex-hippies) that had us look for Jesus in butterflies and release helium balloons out in the parking lot while dressed up like the clown from *Godspell*. In the malaise of pleasantries and feel-good spirituality, or that of force-fed iron-fisted academics, many of us simply failed to learn the true fundamentals of the faith. Throughout grade school and high school, the approach to catechetical instruction and preparation for the sacraments became a matter of passing tests, going through the motions, getting a good grade, and then forgetting what we had learned.

Anyone who was blessed enough to be able to attend a Catholic college may have seen yet another questionable side of religious education. It was not uncommon to have professors who obscenely used their position to push heretical agendas and promote things that were contrary to Church teaching. I know of rogue nuns who taught on the university level and used their class as a soap box to rant and rave about all sorts of crazy personal issues and to pawn off their own brand of new-age pseudo-witchcraft as Catholic spirituality. I know of renegade priests who made it a point to contradict the Church's Sacred Traditions and condemn many of the Church's moral and ethical teachings that they personally didn't like.

As for anyone who attended a secular university, you can bet that they experienced a different kind of faith-rot. Having attended a secular university myself for a few years, I had countless classes in which the professors would bash the Catholic Church and present an extremely biased, false interpretation of the faith and the history of the Church. In other classes, things like sexual promiscuity, homosexual activity, abortion, masturbation, and other soul-destroying filth was presented to us as the acceptable norm that we should be supporting and celebrating.

Within just a few weeks of my first year of college I was subjected to an unbelievable amount of immoral conditioning. All that I knew as being good, decent, right, and wrong, was turned upside down and shoved down an intellectual garbage disposal. If I didn't have at least some conviction and knowledge about my beliefs, I very well might have been swayed by these hijacking hedonists who were supposed to be the ones forming the minds of our nation's future leaders. Those who didn't have a grasp on their faith and who didn't have any spiritual or moral convictions were swept away into an ocean of immoral complacency.

When one adds all this up, along with all the other problems in the Church these days, it's really no wonder people are so lukewarm (at best), confused, turned off, disgusted, and just don't care about their faith. In my opinion, this rampant deterioration of the Catholic faith, and the willful failure to practice it, is rooted in the lack of basic fundamental Church teaching and a severe misunderstanding of it. Many of the would-be faithful have wandered away, have never been taught, or have been dragged away from the solid, foundational, unchanging teachings and beliefs of our Church: beliefs and teachings that were handed on to the apostles from Jesus Christ himself.

The bottom line is that, for a multitude of reasons, we don't know our faith. We can point fingers and suggest culprits, but that still doesn't help the fact that thousands (even millions?) of Catholics don't have a clue about what it truly means to be Catholic. This is a reality that we as a Church need to open our eyes to and face head-on. It is rotting away the core of who we are and what we believe. It is destroying our identity and dignity as a people of God. It's the reason why anti-Catholicism is among the last socially acceptable forms of bigotry. It is severing the relationship that Christ desires to have with each of us individually and collectively as a united people. It is a reality that is ripping the gospel message from our hearts and leaving us spiritually void and vacant, darkened by sin and coerced by the lies of our culture of death.

With so many Catholics not having the slightest grasp of the absolute basics, it is extremely easy to crumble and succumb to a mentality of minimalism, just trying to "be a good person" instead of trying to live a heroic life, rooted in virtue and faith as we are all called to do. How easy it is to be led astray from the truth of Christ and his Church. How easy it is to unwittingly sell our souls to the devil and cruise full-throttle down the highway to hell.

GETTING BACK TO THE "MEAT AND POTATOES" OF OUR FAITH

IT's THE DISREGARDING of the "meat and potatoes" of our faith that has caused such weakness and atrophy in our Church and in our people. We've become spiritually bulimic. We binge on the things in our faith tradition that make us feel good, like the "cuteness" of baptisms, first Communions, and the grandeur of wedding ceremonies, while we purge ourselves of the true meaning and the serious, vital commitment that those things entail. We binge on things like going to Mass on Christmas and Easter and yet never step foot in Church the rest of the year. We binge on things like parish picnics, athletic events, auctions, trivia nights, while we purge ourselves of the true nourishment we need and can get from things like regular Mass attendance, Confession, prayer, adult faith opportunities, retreats, etc. Many in our Church have eaten dessert first and thrown the main course to the dogs. In a word, we're alarmingly malnourished.

As Catholics, we need to go back to the dinner table, pull ourselves up, and dig into a hearty helping of spiritual meat and potatoes. We need to nourish ourselves and feed voraciously on the basic fundamentals of our Catholic faith and redefine the way we live our lives. It's never too late to restore our spiritual health, to take back what we may have lost, or rightfully claim what we may never have received in the first place. But nobody is going to force-feed us. We're big boys and girls now, and we need to take care of ourselves and start eating right!

It's been said again and again that the USA is the greatest mission territory in the world. Some of the neediest people in the world are baptized Catholics who were spiritually abandoned and neglected as soon as the water on their heads dried. Some of the neediest people in the world live in affluent areas and sit in the pews on Sunday mornings. They are there out of a sense of obligation, but have no idea what's going on, and thus fail to go home with a spiritually full stomach. Some of the neediest people are parents who send their kids to Catholic schools and yet make no attempt to back up what their children should be learning at home. Some of the neediest are priests and religious who have long since forgotten the reasons why they were ordained or consecrated.

While it is true that the idea of learning (or relearning) *everything* about one's faith can be intimidating, having a professional-level education and an all-encompassing knowledge of the Church is not necessary to be a good, informed, practicing Catholic. One simply needs the meat and potatoes of the faith to nourish one's soul, enlighten the mind, and motivate one to action.

As the woman who confronted me at that book signing was essentially pointing out, many have given up on trying to educate themselves because so much of the material available is over their heads. After trying to make it through pages of theological jargon written by lofty intellectuals whose office walls are covered in degrees and awards, many simply throw in the towel. And I don't blame them. Many "adult catechesis" classes and books and many Church documents are beautiful, powerful, and immensely rich, but just don't make sense to the average person. Not that the average person is dumb, but rather, those in ivory towers and Vatican offices speak a different language.

THE PURPOSE OF THIS BOOK

JESUS TAUGHT IN A WAY that people could understand. He used images and examples that people were familiar with. That's the beauty of the gospel; it's so simple that a child can understand it, yet so deep that we could study it for the rest of our lives. It's with a similar clarity and simplicity that I hope to present the material in this book. In the chapters and volumes to come, I will cover the fundamentals of faith, Sacred Tradition, liturgy, sacraments, Scripture, prayer, and so on. I will take an honest look at, and address, some of the more unfortunate realities of our Church during these difficult times. I will bring to light such dreaded issues as the priests' sex abuse scandal, gay marriage, abortion, contraception, and stem-cell research. I will challenge the readers to reclaim their faith and to spiritually "put some meat on your bones!" Most importantly, I will do so in a manner that is straightforward, thought provoking, educational, and even enjoyable.

This is not, and will not, be like reading a textbook. That being the case, I wish to note here the sources used in writing this book. Primarily, the theology presented is right out of the *Catechism of the Catholic Church*. The *Catechism* contains the official Church teaching on virtually everything in our Catholic faith.

It draws from Sacred Scripture, Sacred Tradition, the teaching of Church Councils, Canon Law, and other authoritative sources. The *Catechism* is the ultimate book of the meat and potatoes of our faith, but many just can't seem to get though much of it due to its rather complex structure and wording. It's not exactly an easy read.

Other sources that I draw from in this work are the official ritual books that are used for the administration of the sacraments along with the *Old Catholic Encyclopedia* and, of course, my notes from nine years of philosophy and theology classes. To top it off, the reader will notice that I refer quite a bit to the writings and preaching of the late, great Archbishop Fulton J. Sheen. His work is timeless, thought-provoking, and truly inspired. He is a man of God who hit the nail on the head like no other in our modern day. Any other sources that I draw from will be noted as I go along.

So now, without further delay, grab a fork and knife, fill your plate, and get ready for a heaping plate of meat and potatoes Catholicism!

CHAPTER 1

I QUIT!

AS DOCTORS HAVE BEEN telling us for years, exercise is a much needed necessity for overall health. We are designed to be active, and when we are not at least somewhat active for long periods of time, the result is as obvious as the added flabby girth around one's waist and the extra chin, or two, drooping below. Americans more than ever are plagued by the "Dunlop" disease: that's when your belly "done lops" over your belt! With many of today's careers and lifestyles requiring little physical activity, it has become more important than ever to make it a point to get an adequate amount of exercise.

I've always been sort of an athletic guy, not so much that I played lots of organized sports and had an intense interest in them, but I've always enjoyed physical activity. As a youngster (before the days of intellectually enslaving home video games) I'd do all the usual things that kids did: roller skate, swim, ride bikes, play tag, shoot baskets, play wiffle ball, cut grass (with a push mower), pull weeds (with bare hands, not a fancy weed whacker), and the other many activities that kept us occupied, in shape, and out of trouble, for the most part. I did play some organized sports such as little league baseball and soccer, but I was quickly turned off by the crazed, overbearing coaches and parents who felt the fate of mankind rested upon our beating the dreaded Burger

World Bandits, or whoever our opposing team of the day happened to be.

When I got into high school, I was a pole-vaulter on the track team my freshman year, but that came to an end as I was finally able to pursue my longtime interest of weight lifting. Inspired by memories of Lou Ferrigno as the Incredible Hulk (my favorite childhood TV show) I wanted to bulk up to 330 pounds and be able to flip over cars and smash down brick buildings. Well, I did eventually bulk up to 240 or so, but I'm still having trouble flipping over those cars and smashing through brick walls.

My only other serious athletic pursuit was cycling when I was in junior high. My dad and my brother were serious cyclists, so I naturally got involved, too. I decked out my rather cheap, clumsy ten-speed with all the gadgets that were supposed to make it more aerodynamic, and I, of course, added a little on-board computer to tell me how fast I was going and how many miles I rode. Then I naturally had to get all the fancy cycling clothes, which I always did feel a bit funny riding around in. After getting geared up and looking like I was ready for the Tour de France, I began my short-lived career. I'd go out on 20- to 30-mile rides on a weekly basis, and occasionally for 40 or 50, but after awhile I began to lose interest. Sure, I was in great shape and could ride like the wind, but it just didn't spark enough excitement to keep my attention. But before I hung up my riding shorts for one last time, I decided to enter a triathlon that was to take place at the end of the summer.

It was a triathlon designed for kids in the seventh and eighth grades, but it was nonetheless very challenging. In the beginning of the summer I'd been reading triathlon magazines and watching the *Ironman* (the mother of all triathlons) on TV, so I had a little extra motivation to keep me going. I was still doing my 20- to 40-mile bike rides, and I also ran pretty frequently at the time as part of my training. To top it off, I was spending a lot of time at the pool, though mostly just lazing around in the water like a beach bum. Life was great, and I had no apprehensions or fear about doing well in this triathlon. As a matter of fact, I thought that I might even win it.

As those hot summer days progressed, I knew that I should probably really get down to business and start actually training more intensely for the rapidly approaching day of the event. But still filled with an extreme overconfidence, I did the exact opposite and just kind of took it easy as the rest of the summer went by. In fact, that ended up being the laziest summer of my life. I had a job cutting grass, but when I wasn't doing that, I just sat around and ate Twinkies and drank Pepsi all day (and I had to do so secretly, as no junk food was allowed in the house)! The only exercise I got, besides cutting grass, was riding my bike to the 7-Eleven to play Pac Man, drink Slurpees, and stock up on hot dogs. I had a theory in which I thought all that "heavy fuel" would turn me into a powerful diesel engine and give me even more of an edge in crushing my competition!

Finally, the big day of the triathlon came, and I was still under the great delusion that I would dominate the event! And so, fueled by convenience store junk food, I made my way to the pool for the swimming phase of the race. As I eyeballed my competition, I noticed most of them were in pretty good shape. I also noticed how badly out of shape I'd become. My once six pack of abs were now covered in flab, and squishy fat was hanging over the edge of my swim trunks. But again, I convinced myself that it would be to my advantage. All that fat and blubber would help me float better and give me the ability to blast through the water like a great and mighty Arctic walrus! Right?

I waddled into position at the starting line and at the sound of the shot I leaped into the pool and swam as fast as humanly possible. I kicked my lethargic legs as hard as I could and flung my flabby arms like an out-of-control windmill. The water was thrashing all around me as the yells and cheers of the crowd got louder and louder. "I must really be kicking butt," I thought to myself. "I've got this thing in the bag ... just give me my trophy and I'll go home right now!" I must admit, as I swam my last lap in the pool, I was absolutely exhausted. When I finished my swim and cleared the chlorine out of my eyes, I was shocked and horrified to find that I was the second to last person out of the pool! My overinflated confidence suddenly burst like those overcooked bratwursts I'd been eating all summer long.

Knowing that I needed to make up some serious time, I scampered over to my bike, got on it, and started pedaling as fast as I could. With every revolution of my wheels, I got more and more light-headed. I felt sick. As I huffed and puffed and tried desperately to pedal my fat butt around the course, the other kids in the race were whizzing by me so speedily that it made me dizzy. I picked up a little time on the bike, but not much. And just when I thought things were as bad as they could get, it came time for the most dreaded part of the race: the running phase.

Even though I did do a little running now and then, I've always hated it, and trying to run after already being on the verge of collapse just didn't work too well. I ran for a few minutes, trying desperately to summon up any last remnants of strength and energy, and then I just gave up. I made the conscious decision to quit. I simply walked through the final portion of the race. All around, people were cheering me on and encouraging me to keep going, but I just didn't care. I didn't even try anymore. My endurance was shot. By the time I crossed the finish line, I was utterly humiliated. I hung my head low in shame and disgust. All those hours of eating hot dogs and Twinkies, sitting on the couch watching Kung Fu movies, and hanging out at 7-Eleven playing video games flashed before my eyes and mocked me. But, of course, I had no one to blame but myself. My severe lack of endurance and incredibly pathetic athletic display was my own doing.

It was the first time in my life that I simply quit something, that I purposely gave up, that I shamefully threw in the towel. What a terrible feeling: To abandon the mission out of sheer humiliation and lack of will, to jump ship because of my own laziness and lack of preparation. To give up because I no longer cared or because the possibility of being first was crushed. It was a devastating blow to my adolescent ego.

As we all know, quitting something that is bad, such as smoking, drinking excessively, etc., is a good thing, but quitting something that is beneficial and constructive is not so good. Every year on January 1, hundreds of thousands of people make resolutions to do good things: to lose weight, to get fit, and to make various improvements in their lives. And as always, many start out in a very gung-ho fashion and keep their resolutions for a few months, only to fizzle out or just plain quit. And Lord knows we all have lots of excuses for quitting — "I don't have the time ... I don't have the energy ... I'm not seeing any difference or results ..." and so on.

It is truly heartbreaking to see good people give up and quit things, no matter how challenging those things may be. I'm sure we all know people who have given up on their marriages, their families, their careers, their vocations. In many of those cases, we say to ourselves, "What's wrong with him/her/them? I can't believe they're giving up! He/she/they could work this out if they really tried." Although we don't know what is entirely in the mind and heart of a quitter, it boils down to one thing: being overwhelmed and frustrated to the point of simply giving up and giving in.

ADDRESSING THE REASONS PEOPLE QUIT THE CHURCH

AS WE ALL KNOW, we can make excuses and rationalize and justify almost anything if we work hard enough at it, especially our reasons for quitting something. Joseph Goebbels, Adolph Hitler's minister of propaganda, is attributed with the saying, "If a lie is repeated enough times, it will become widely accepted as truth." No doubt about it, we often use this tactic on ourselves. We lie to ourselves to the point that we finally embrace it as the truth. And make no mistake, the "master of lies" (Satan) is always behind it.

As a priest, it's always very sad when I hear of couples getting divorced or separating. It's very disheartening when I hear of someone leaving the priesthood or the consecrated life. But the thing that I (and I'm sure all priests) hear about the most is people leaving their faith and/or leaving the Church. When we hear about marriages and families falling apart because of abuse or neglect, it's not too hard to understand and sympathize with the reasons people start considering divorce — although, working through those "bad times" (that couples committed to in their wedding vows) in order to bring about healing and peace is the reality that should be taken seriously.

When we hear of priests or religious having nervous breakdowns, falling into depression or addiction because of the overwhelming challenges of their vocation (which most folks have no idea about), it's not very difficult to cut them some slack, although again, they too are called to carry those "Good Friday" crosses and keep their commitment to help bring about the new life of Easter Sunday. But as a priest, when I hear the reasons many people come up with for leaving the Church and flushing their faith down the toilet, I can't help but to shake my head in disbelief.

Here are some of the most common excuses I hear:

- The lady in the pew behind me gave me a mean look at Mass one day when my baby was crying.
- The Athletic Association at my parish wouldn't let my child be on her friend's team.
- The fourth grade teacher of the parish school yelled at my daughter.
- My neighbor goes to that parish, and I can't stand him!
- The Church hates women! (At the same time, others accuse us of worshipping Mary.)
- The parish council wouldn't let me run the beer booth at the parish picnic.
- Father is too liberal.
- Father is too conservative.
- Father is too boring.
- The music is lousy.
- One of the ladies in the quilters group said something mean to my grandmother.
- I can't stand all those pious devotions.
- I don't agree with the Church's teaching on this or that.
- The pastor never did get that front door fixed.
- I can't stand all those coffee and doughnut socials.
- The archbishop is a mean, mean man.
- There shouldn't be girl Mass servers.
- Those Lenten fish fries stink up the parish hall too much.
- Father wouldn't do our wedding (which was to take place at the zoo).
- We had to take a class before our child could be baptized.
- My son wasn't allowed to wear his Scooby-Doo tie at his First Holy Communion.

- My daughter was told to go home and put on a different dress (one that actually covered her up) before her Confirmation.
- Every time I come to church they ask me for money.
- The Church wants me to vote a certain way on a certain issue.
- Father refused to let us play a Guns N' Roses song at my brother's funeral.

And so, "To heck with the Catholic Church and all this religion stuff!"

Many say it's not so much their religion that they have given up on and abandoned, but *organized* religion: the Church. Keep in mind my friends, that when one studies the nature and history of God's revelation to mankind, in the proper context, it is quite clear that God chose to reveal himself and his plan of salvation in an *organized* manner. For that matter, all of God's creation is organized. From the changing of the seasons to the intricate workings of the tiniest of critters, it's all incredibly organized which, in and of itself, gives glory and witness to God.

Then, of course, there are naturally more serious issues that persuade people to leave the Church. Some point at the Church's vast real estate, artwork, historical treasures, and apparent wealth as a hypocrisy that should be condemned:

- Why isn't all that money given to the poor?
- Why doesn't the Church sell all its treasures and help others with the profits?
- Isn't that what Jesus would have done?

First of all, yes, the Catholic Church does have many treasures and loads of real estate. The Catholic Church owns and operates more schools, hospitals, health care services, social service organizations, and churches (of course) than any other organization in the world! All of the Church's real estate is there to benefit and serve the people of God. It belongs to the people, it is run by the people (under the Church's supervision), and it is for the people. And yes, it takes a truckload of money to run these things. And Lord knows there are oodles of troubles that come along with trying to manage and run them efficiently and properly.

Let me tell you, by the way, that I don't know many parishes and Church-run organizations that are not struggling financially to make ends meet. In the grand scheme of things, there is much more poverty in the Church than there is wealth. Many of the riches that are associated with the Catholic Church, in fact, do not even belong to her anymore. Take, for example, the great cathedral of Notre Dame in Paris. It is owned by the French government. And if you ever get a chance to visit Rome and see the Sistine Chapel, don't bother trying to take pictures of the artwork — it's prohibited by the Japanese television corporation. They became owners of the copyrights in exchange for picking up the tab for the restoration, which the Vatican could not afford.

In regard to the Church's wealth in the form of artwork, cathedrals, and historical treasures (that she does still own), that too has ultimately come from the people of God in order to give praise and thanksgiving to God. The incredible works of art, musical compositions, architecture, and craftsmanship that is seen and experienced in the Church's ceremonies and buildings is all for the glory of God and is there to enrich the worship of the people. For many folks, their only exposure to such things has come from the Church, and they have willingly given for that purpose. It is there for everybody to enjoy and experience, and that is why these things are so valiantly safeguarded.

For many, the only place of peace and solitude and heavenly escape from the chaos of modern life is found in their church or cathedral. That was the whole point in designing and building them in the first place. When one walks into a huge, ornate place of worship, it is supposed to be a taste of heaven, a sanctuary on earth, and a special dwelling place for and with the Lord.

It's an indisputable fact that Catholic organizations have raised, and continue to donate, millions upon millions of dollars for the poor, the sick, and the needy, while still giving them a beautiful place to come and worship. The Church is a place millions of people from all walks of life, of all social status, of all races and places lovingly call home. Sure, we could rip down our churches and cathedrals and sell all the Church's treasures to help others; we could also sell the Statue of Liberty, the original copy of the Constitution, or all the things in our museums to pay off the national debt and help the poor of our country. But in doing that, we'd also be ripping down and selling who we are as a people: our heritage, our tradition, our legacy. We'd be selling our souls in a way. Now, if it was absolutely necessary to sell these things to solve the world's problems, it would be another story, but it is not. Jesus never suggested selling the Temple to help the poor who also worshiped there. "The poor you will always have with you," our Lord tells us, and there is a more obvious solution to helping them.

Hunger, homelessness, poverty, and virtually every human need that continues to go unmet is largely due to selfishness, corruption, and greed. America is a country of both extreme poverty and obscene wealth. Those who complain about how others should give away all their wealth are the same ones who often give little or nothing to help or assist those in need. It's always somebody else's responsibility to pick up the tab and pay the bills. I have no doubt that the needs of our world could easily be met (while still safeguarding our national and religious heirlooms) if *everybody* was willing to help just a little instead of expecting one or two organizations to do all the work. All humanity suffers the hardships of selfishness and sin, and all humanity could alleviate those hardships if we *all* pitched in.

Another big and very serious issue that motivates people to leave the Church and abandon their faith these days is the clergy sex abuse scandal. No doubt it is sickening! For a man of God to sexually abuse the innocent of the Lord's flock is an abomination that cries to heaven for justice! For the Church's bishops to do little or nothing, or even seemingly protect the abuser, is horrific to say the least! The facts should be faced: Yes, some bishops have made huge mistakes in dealing with this terrible situation. Yes, there are some priests who are very ill and have committed crimes for which they should be held accountable. However, the psychologists and mental health professionals upon whose counsel and recommendations many bishops based their actions in dealing with sick priests should also be held accountable.

Some other facts that should be taken into consideration are these: A recent investigation by the John Jay College of Criminal Justice experts discovered that what the Church is dealing with is a crisis of abuse of teen males, not attacks on prepubescent children. Eighty-one percent of the clergy abuse is homosexual predation, which obviously is also a horrible evil that must be rooted out. Another fact that is so blatantly overlooked is that the vast majority of child abusers in the world are not celibate clergymen, but people who are married, who are parents, and who come from all walks of life.

The reason that so many bishops are extra cautious in dealing with alleged abusive priests is because they are just that: *alleged*. There are lots and lots of false allegations being made in hopes of scoring financial restitution. The media is always quick to put in the headlines, "Priest Is Accused of Sexual Misconduct." What happens again and again though, which the public never (or rarely) hears about, is what you'll see in the back page of the newspaper a few weeks later, written in tiny print, "Priest Found Innocent of Allegations."

Something else we see quite often with this issue is men who either left or were booted from the priesthood years ago who then later went on to abuse, and yet the media still calls them "priests." All that being said, though, a priest who is found guilty should obviously face the legal consequences like any other criminal. And that, too, one rarely hears about. The media seem to print mostly stories that involve "alleged abuse" and what seems like a sneaky cover-up by Church officials.

But make no mistake, again, there are sick men who have used and abused the Church and hidden behind a collar to hurt others. There have been men who have made terrible mistakes in trying to deal with these individuals. The damage they have done has not only hurt their victims but the entire Christian community and Christ himself. But the questions remain: Is the Church as a whole corrupt because of these imprudent and very sick men? Absolutely not! Is the mission of the Church in vain because of the mistakes of a minority of individuals? I certainly don't think so.

WE MUST STAY!

THE REALITY IS THAT there are serious problems going on within the Church as with any other organization on earth, and there will always be. We could easily wage war on the institution of marriage and parenthood because some spouses and parents are abusive and fail to do their duty. We could condemn our law enforcement organizations who are supposed to be "protecting and serving" while corruption runs wild within. Should we abandon medical help because of the mockery and disgrace of doctors who are supposed to be healing, but are instead filling their pockets by killing the unborn and elderly and maiming vanity-obsessed people?

There is clearly much corruption in our government and within our country, but are we going to leave it? Are not the principles that our nation was founded upon worth fighting for in the face of corruption? How quickly we forget that evil dwells within the individual human heart, not in any one particular group or institution. And yes, the evil of those individuals can certainly penetrate any organization on earth, even one founded by the Son of God. But this is certainly no reason to quit! It's a battle cry to rise up and purify the ranks and cleanse the filth and corruption that has taken effect, and this is something that will take time.

The fact that the Church has grown and flourished despite the ungodly evils that she has suffered throughout the centuries, and the fact that she has continued to be a source of grace and inspiration for millions of people for over 2,000 years (the longest running organization in the history of the world) is a sure sign that God is ultimately in charge despite the human weakness and stupid (and criminal) things that those who are in positions of leadership have done. As Archbishop Fulton Sheen once stated, "The Church is like a hospital. There is often pus, blood, vermin, sickness, and screams, but there is also healing, knowledge, and love."

In looking at the big picture now, and considering all the many excuses folks come up with to leave the Church, ask yourself: Is it Jesus' fault that your son got put on a different soccer team, that the lady in the pew behind you gave you a dirty look, that your son's teacher has a bad temper, that you got upset due to your own lack of understanding about the faith or what it takes to pay the bills of a large parish or run a diocese? Is it Jesus' fault that individuals within the Church and within any parish on earth are at times stubborn, misguided, arrogant, uncharitable, condescending, lazy, or just plain stupid? As long as we human beings remain able to exercise free will, we will do good things that make people happy and bad things that make people mad and sometimes hurt them.

As a priest, I can tell you that I, too, get aggravated with a lot of things that go on in the Church. Some of my brother priests have done things that fill me with a holy rage, and to be perfectly honest with you, many others I just plain don't get along with (though I still love and pray for them). Some of my parishioners, and many of the things that go on in parish life, can be a source of nonstop frustration and headaches. Some of the Church's personal devotions and spiritual traditions can seem overly pious to some, and they certainly don't appeal to everybody, and that's okay.

Pious personal devotions come and go. Annoying priests and imprudent bishops come and go. Aggravating parishioners come and go. Disagreements and scandals come and go. Bad vibes, hurt feelings, and differences of opinion will come and go. But hold on tight, because the grace of God that he gives us so abundantly in the sacraments (through those same priests we may not like) *will not* come and go. The message of conversion, hope, and joy that we receive in the gospel *will not* come and go. God's love for us, the mercy of Jesus Christ, and the need to work together and overcome our differences as a united people of God *will not* come and go. Jesus needs you! His Church needs you!

WHAT IS THE CHURCH?

LET'S TAKE A MOMENT TO consider the nature of the Church as a foundation of further understanding. For starters, another good quote from Archbishop Fulton Sheen states, "There are not more than 100 people in the world who truly hate the Catholic Church, but there are millions who hate what *they perceive* the Catholic Church to be." How true this is. A real crisis today among would-be-faithful Catholics, as well as non-Catholics, is that they are getting their information about what the Church teaches and why she teaches it from people and sources who hate the Church! No wonder so many are confused and mislead. Ignorance leads to hatred, and this has certainly happened with the Church.

I don't know how many times I've seen headlines in notoriously anti-Christian/Catholic newspapers, magazines, or news shows that proclaim in big, bold print, "Catholic Church Condemns . . . (fill in the blank)!" Naturally, the reaction to this is enraged, instant disgust that emotionally repels the reader from then finding out why the Church has actually condemned something (if she even truly has). But even then, so much of the information that is given by these sources is biased, skewed, and manipulated in ways that do not tell people the truth about what the Church is saying. Thus, the vital importance of getting information about the Church from *the Church*, not from the *enemies* of the Church!

So what does the Church say about herself? Well, she says all kinds of things, but a couple a key statements are these:

> "It was the Son's task to accomplish the Father's plan of salvation in the fullness of time. Its accomplishment was the reason for his being sent. The Lord Jesus inaugurated his Church by preaching the Good News, that is, the coming of the Reign of God, promised over the ages in the Scriptures. To fulfill the Father's will, Christ ushered in the kingdom of heaven on earth. The Church is the Reign of Christ already present in mystery." (CCC 763)

And,

> "The Church, in Christ, is like a sacrament a sign and instrument, that is, of communion with God and of unity among all men" ["men" here includes women, of course]. The Church's first purpose is to be the sacrament of the

inner union of men with God. Because men's communion with one another is rooted in that union with God, the Church is also the sacrament of the *unity of the human race.* In her, this unity is already begun, since she gathers men "from every nation, from all tribes and peoples and tongues"; at the same time, the Church is the "sign and instrument" of the full realization of the unity yet to come. (CCC 775)

So what does all this mean? It means that Jesus founded his Church to be the vehicle for salvation, for unity with God and each other for all people of all places for all time. As our Lord says, "I am the way, and the truth, and the life; no one comes to the Father, but by me" (John 14:6). The Church is the place where we then learn about that "way." It's the place where we receive that "truth." We are then empowered by God's grace to live and experience the fullness of that "life."

As you've noticed by now, the Church is always referred to as "she." This is because the Church is considered the "Bride of Christ." In Scripture we hear Jesus referring to himself as the bridegroom and the Church as his bride; it is a spousal relationship. Jesus loves his bride with a total self-sacrificing love. He laid down his life for her (for us) and provides for her (our) needs with the gospel and the sacraments. Jesus will never leave his bride. In Matthew 16:18, we hear, "I will build my church, and the powers of death shall not prevail against it." So despite the failings of sinful men, the Church will always remain a source of life, nourishment, and salvation.

It's important for us as Catholics to realize that our Church is the only one established by Jesus Christ himself. The Eastern Orthodox churches broke away from unity with the Pope in 1054. The multitude of protestant churches all have their roots in the Reformation, which started in 1517. Martin Luther got the ball rolling, and though he certainly did bring up things that needed to be addressed (many that eventually were), he ultimately broke from the Church and began his own. And so that precedent followed. Whenever people became disgruntled with their new churches, they "protested," left, and began their own. If one looks in the telephone directory for churches, it is evident that there are many, many different branches of "Christian" churches, and all of them are offshoots of other protestant churches.

It is only the Catholic Church that can be historically, factually traced back to Jesus Christ himself. Our bishops and popes can all be traced back in direct lineage, with unbroken succession, to St. Peter (the first Pope) and the apostles. In Matthew 16:18-19, we hear Jesus tell Simon,

> "And I tell you, you are Peter, and upon this rock I will build my church, and the powers of death shall not prevail against it. I will give you the keys to the kingdom of heaven, and whatever you bind on earth shall be bound in heaven, and whatever you loose on earth shall be loosed in heaven."

There are a number of important things to consider in this passage. First of all, Jesus changes Simon's name to Peter (*Kephas*), which in Aramaic means "a massive rock." And so, there is no mistake that Jesus built his Church on the foundation, the "rock," of Peter. Secondly, notice that Jesus said, "I will build *my* church." He didn't say, "*your* church," or "*a* church," but "*my* church." We do not have the right to change the church that Jesus founded according to our own likes and dislikes. We simply do not have the authority to do so. And so while various nonsacred traditions, disciplines, and practices of the Church have changed and gone through developments, the doctrines of the faith, which Jesus himself gave us, do not and cannot change.

Thirdly, in this passage from Matthew we see that Jesus specifically gave Peter the position as the primary leader and teacher of his Church on earth. The "keys of the kingdom" and the authority to "bind and loose" were given to Peter to carry on Christ's role as the Shepherd of the Church. It is the pope's task to keep the Church unified, nourished, and in line with the teaching of Jesus.

And so then, the Church that Jesus founded on the rock of Peter (the pope) and the leadership of the apostles (the bishops) is ultimately about expressing Christ's love for us and making it real. It's about us as the people of God, the family of believers, expressing our love for him and living out the full gospel message that he gave us. The Church exists to help us grow as the "Body" of Christ and becoming more united as a community of believers. Don't forget, Jesus didn't come for *me*, he came for *we*!

Jesus promised his followers that he would be with them always, and he continues to be real and present in our lives and in our world by means of his word and the sacraments, which we experience in the Church. This is why our Catholic faith is based on Scripture *and* Sacred Tradition (which differ from nonsacred tradition). Sacred Tradition is the (initially) unwritten Christian doctrine that is based on the teaching authority that the apostles of Jesus handed on directly to their successors to be safeguarded, and continued to be handed down to future generations. This is essentially the primary job of the Magisterium (bishops, cardinals, and so on): to keep the teachings and doctrines of the faith free from error, and often dangerous, personal interpretation.

Obviously, Scripture is of the utmost importance to our faith, but it is necessary to remember that the Bible itself is the product of Sacred Tradition. The Bible (as we know it, especially the New Testament) is the product of the Church — she wrote and produced it (under the inspiration of the Holy Spirit), not the other way around. There are many things that Catholics (and other Christian denominations) do and believe in regard to the practice of their faith (such as items in the liturgy and sacramental preparation and reception) that are only referred to briefly (if at all) in Scripture, but have been written about and taught from the days of the post-Pentecost Christian communities. And there are plenty of sources to read about such things (for example, the writings of the early Church Fathers), all of which, again, can be traced in direct succession back to Jesus and the apostles.

One could spend a lifetime studying the intricacies and theology of the Church. Volumes upon volumes have been written explaining the nature of the Church and her historical progressions and developments. That being said, I'll stop here and get back to the original point, which is that people are leaving the Church for the wrong reasons. They are "throwing the baby out with the bathwater," as the old saying goes.

THE CHURCH IS OUR HOME

THE CHURCH, AS AN INSTITUTION, as a place of worship, and as a family of believers, is our home. It is where Christ is truly present. It is where he continues to lead us, teach us, heal us, and nourish us. It is where we experience his love in a multitude of ways. It is where we, as God's family, are challenged to work through our disputes and arguments instead of just moving out and moving on, which only brings more separation and pain to everyone.

Sometimes the roof of our home has a few leaks, and so we need to patch them. Sometimes it may be a bit cold inside, and so we need to turn up the furnace. At times our home blows a fuse, but the power is still there. Our faucet might get tarnished and rusty, but the water coming out of it is still pure and clean. The weeds in our front yard need pulling every now and again and the over-grown bushes can use a good trimming. The windows get dirty, and we need to clean them to let more light in and we need to open them up to let the fresh air in. Yes, our beloved homes need upkeep and work, but despite the challenges, it would be foolish to simply pack up, leave, and burn them to the ground.

Our homes give us shelter from the raging storms. They give us comfort after a long day of work. The home is the center of our lives. It is where we gather with family and friends and where we share meals and memories. It is where we work together, learn from each other, and practice virtue and discipline. It is from where we go and to where we return. It is our castle and our sanctuary. The "home" of our Church is the same. It is where we belong, and we should not let anything or anyone drive us away. And if we have, then it's time to take it back, to rediscover the beauty, the richness, and the meaning of our home, the Church. It's time to take ownership of our home, to come back inside, sit down at the table with the family, and dig into a big ol' plate of... you guessed it... meat and potatoes!

CHAPTER 2

SHOW ME A SIGN!

IF YOU'VE READ MY previous book, *Hunting for God, Fishing for the Lord,* I don't have to tell you how much I passionately love the outdoors and how much it has contributed to my quality of life — physically, mentally, and, most importantly, spiritually. Much of the time I spend in the outdoors is primarily a solitary venture: just I, my bow and arrow, fishing rod, or camera, the beauty of creation, and God Almighty. It's a time to relish the peace and quiet and the prayerful communion with the Lord. It renews and refreshes my soul in an indescribable manner — not to mention, such activities also put healthy, fresh food on the table while instilling a greater sense of stewardship for the land and a respect for what one eats.

Where I tend to differ from a lot of folks who enjoy hunting, fishing, and the outdoors is that whereas many will spend the better part of a morning and evening in the woods or on the water, I'll spend the entire day (when time allows), sunup till sundown, with no break whatsoever. I simply love being out there that much! People say I'm crazy and that I'm wasting my time doing things like bass fishing when it's 105 degrees or deer hunting in the middle of the afternoon, but I don't care. And in fact, almost every year I see the biggest buck of the season right in the middle of the day when everybody else is back taking a nap or watching football.

There is one particular piece of land that I've been hunting now for well over a decade. It's a very rugged, hilly chunk of woods that is extremely thick and dense with mature trees and tight brush. Over the years I've come to know the area like the back of my hand. I'm keenly aware of, and make mental notes about, remarkable animal tracks and other signs that show up in certain areas. One particular spring as I finished out the final day of turkey hunting for the season, I noticed a huge set of deer tracks along the bottom of a steep ridge. These tracks were so big and so intriguing that I decided to purchase a trail camera to try and get a few pictures of the deer that so prominently left his mark. A trail camera is basically a device that one sets up along a deer trail or in other areas where wildlife activity has been evident, and by means of a motion detector, the camera snaps a few pictures when triggered. It's a fun way to monitor *exactly* what is roaming the woods.

Well, the trail camera I purchased was a very inexpensive model, and after one use it broke. And out of that one use, I only got two pictures, but those two pictures were of the massive buck that was in the area! I couldn't believe my eyes! This buck was huge! His body looked like a thoroughbred race horse: tall, sleek, fast, and muscular. It was still late spring, so his antlers were not fully grown yet (bucks shed and regrow them every year), but I could tell that this buck was going to have a magnificent, kingly crown upon his head when fall came around.

With the knowledge of that deer in the area and more and more signs showing up as the season got closer, you can imagine (especially if you're a hunter) how frantically excited I was! As the season got underway, I was seeing a fair amount of does and small bucks but no sign of the big dude. Did he leave the area? Did someone take him already? Hmmm. My mind began to ponder various scenarios that would explain his disappearance.

A few more weeks had passed, and still there was no sign of the big buck. Thinking he was gone, I began to focus my efforts on harvesting a nice large doe to fill the freezer instead, although she wouldn't provide nearly as much meat as that huge buck would have. One particular day as the morning was slowly evolving into afternoon, I was comfortably sitting aloft in my tree stand, reflecting on the beauty of the morning and the exciting encounter I had earlier with a small buck, when all of a sudden I saw a little movement through the brush way down on the other end of the creek bed. Suddenly the movement got faster, and I heard an approaching ruckus of splashing water and displaced gravel. Lo and behold, here he came trotting down the edge of the creek, in the middle of the afternoon! It was he!

As the titanic beast of a buck came by my tree stand, I made a little grunting sound to get him to stop. And sure enough he did stop for a second. I was in shock! Here at 45 yards was without a doubt the most incredible, beautiful, majestic, massive buck with the biggest set of antlers I had ever seen in the wild in all my life! This was the kind of deer you'd see on magazine and book covers or in wildlife paintings and videos. As he was too far away for a good shot with my bow, all I could do was sit back and watch in awe as he quickly moved on across the creek and up the hill. After he was gone, I let out a deep breath of pent-up jubilation and began to shake from the nerve-rattling excitement.

Wow! And again I say, *wow!* Just to see a completely wild animal of that caliber is a rare treat. That kind of encounter inspires dreams for years to come. It was a scene I'll never forget. What a gift to just witness such an elusive creature in all his glory. It was a truly awesome experience! As I mentioned earlier, every year I see the biggest deer during times when everybody else has given up. It really is amazing what one can experience by simply being vigilant, by keeping one's eyes and ears open and persevering. And this applies to everything in life, especially our spiritual lives.

Just like many a deer hunter, we can put in a minimum amount of time in our relationship with God, and then just kind of give up and move on, all the while missing out on what may have been a true encounter with the divine. For many, in regards to their spiritual lives, they go to church on Sunday, say a few prayers throughout the week, and then just fall asleep to the reality and presence of God and completely ignore him until disaster or hardship strikes.

GOD'S SIGNS

MOST PEOPLE OF FAITH can recount at least one time in their lives when they experienced a very real and incredibly powerful manifestation of God. Perhaps it was the birth of a child or an important prayer being answered in an extraordinarily obvious manner. Those are things that instantly open our eyes and ears to the reality of God working in our lives. They are things that we should never forget, but as time goes on, we actually do start to forget the impact of those experiences. And as more time passes, we once again start to doubt, and we start to put demanding expectations on God. If God really exists, we want him to make his presence known in big, dramatic ways. We want him to show us a sign, when and how we want it manifested. And if he doesn't meet our demands, we convince ourselves that he's not listening, that he doesn't care, and that perhaps he doesn't exist after all. We condition ourselves to ignore the obvious.

As we hear in Scripture, failing to recognize the obvious is something that happened to many people who encountered Jesus. All throughout the gospel we hear of Jesus miraculously healing those who are sick, raising people from the dead, giving sight to the blind, walking on water, driving out demons, and yet people always seemed to come up with an excuse not to recognize this clear manifestation of God's work. "This guy can't be the son of God, he must be a magician, or possessed, or something," people said. Again and again, many failed to recognize the signs God was leaving through his Son, Jesus.

As Catholics, we too can have that same difficulty recognizing Jesus. We can fall into that same trap of failing to look for him in the most recognizable, obvious places. We can spend years longing to experience the mercy and forgiveness of God, and yet forget that the sacrament of Reconciliation (that Jesus gave us) is available every week. We can read book after book about spirituality, trying to figure out who God is and what he's all about, and yet forget to open and read the most important book of all: the Bible.

In those times when we desperately need the presence of Jesus in our lives to get us through whatever it is we're struggling with, we often forget that he is present to us — Body, Blood, Soul, and Divinity — in the Eucharist, in the tabernacle or monstrance at a church or adoration chapel near us. When we wonder whether God really loves us, we forget to gaze upon the crucifix and take to heart the brutal reality of what he did for us as the ultimate act of love. Throughout our daily lives when things are going wrong, when everything seems to be working against us, and when we are at our wits' end, we so often fail to recognize how God is there with us, reaching out to help us and comfort us through others.

There is a story I heard once that makes the point very well: There was a man who lived in a small river town that was being overtaken by a flood. As the water rose, everyone evacuated the town and got to higher, safer ground until the waters subsided. This one particular man, however, did not evacuate. When asked why, he was quick to say, "I have faith in the Lord! He will not abandon me!" And so the waters continued to rise, but still the man remained. As he sat on his front porch, a jeep came barreling down the soon-to-be-submerged street. It stopped in front of his house, and the driver yelled to the man on the porch, "Quick, get in! You don't have much time!" Again, the man refused the help and said, "No thank you. I have faith in the Lord! He will not abandon me!" And so the jeep moved on.

Alas, the water still kept rising, and soon it was covering the streets and had overtaken the man's porch. And so he climbed up on the roof of his house and waited out the looming catastrophe. Suddenly, a boat came sputtering up the flooded street and stopped in front of the man's house. The boat driver hollered to the man, "Hurry up and get in the boat! I'll get you to safety! You don't have much time left!" True to form, the man yelled back down to the boat captain, "Thanks, but no thanks. The Lord will save me." Shaking his head in amazed disbelief, the captain trolled on by and left.

The water was now over the roof and all the way up to the man's waist. Out of nowhere, a helicopter came chopping through the darkened sky and began hovering over the nearly drowned man. A rescue ladder dropped from the helicopter down to the man and a voice commanded from a megaphone, "Climb up! Climb up now!" In the midst of all the noise and commotion of wind, rain, and loud, spinning helicopter blades, the man screamed back his final words, "God will save me!" And with that, the helicopter flew away. Soon after, the man drowned as he was swept away by the violent flood waters.

The next thing he knew, the man was suddenly standing before St. Peter at the gates of heaven. Very upset and angry, he says to St. Peter, "All right, I need to talk to God. Where is he!?" Slowly and reverently, St. Peter ushers the man into the presence of the Almighty. The man runs up to God without hesitation and begins interrogating him: "Why didn't you help me down there!? What's wrong with you!? Here I was witnessing for you and trying to set an example for others with my faith and you let me drown! You made an absolute fool out of me, and it didn't do much to help your image either! Why!?" After the man had finished with his enraged and troubled statement, God just shook his head and replied to the man, "You idiot! I sent you a jeep, a boat, and a helicopter! What more did you want!?"

The moral of the story, of course, is that the Lord is constantly reaching out to us in many obvious ways, but we constantly fail to recognize them because it's not exactly what we wanted or expected. God manifests himself and leaves us his sign in things like the simple daily blessings he bestows upon us that we, again, fail to recognize or to thank him for. His sign comes in the form of his creation. To think that the amazing complexity and beauty of created things, that the intricate, ingenious working of the mind and body of both humans and animals, is some kind of ongoing miraculous mistake is absolutely absurd, in my opinion. How foolish and blind can one be? To think that everything came from nothing is not only scientifically impossible, but it is also a slap in the omnipotent face of God Almighty.

God leaves us his signs everywhere. Yet, isn't it amazing how we fail to make the connection and see the big picture? Going back to the story of that magnificent buck I encountered on that magical autumn afternoon, even though I had a picture of that deer and I did eventually see him with my own eyes, I knew he was there months before that personal interaction. The huge tracks he left behind everywhere he went made it clear he was in the area. The stout trees and thick shrubs he was ripping to shreds with his antlers as the rut approached gave witness to the fact that this was not some little immature buck. The violently scraped-up dirt and large, matted-down areas of grass where he was bedding were clear signs to me of his presence. I never once doubted that deer's existence. I didn't have to see to believe. To think all those signs were some kind of magical, natural mistake made by something else would have been utter foolishness!

As I mentioned, one of the ways that God leaves his signs and works in our lives is through each other — we are made in his image and likeness. The love, kindness, mercy, generosity, and guidance of others are clear signs of his work and presence in our lives. Being made in the "image and likeness of God" means that we are made by a loving God for the purpose of loving him and one another. We are to be reflections of that self-sacrificing love of Christ, no matter what our state in life may be. God often uses us to be his guiding light for others, and much of the time we don't even realize it. Then of course, there are those moments when God manifests himself in ways that are the most obvious of all, those "God-incidences," as a friend of mine likes to call them. Those are the times when things happen that are so plainly of God that we'd simply have to be a complete and total idiot not to recognize them as God's handiwork.

GOD IN SCRIPTURE — *SOMETHING* HAPPENED!

BUT THE PRIMARY WAY that God leaves his sign in our lives is through his Church, his word, and the sacraments that he gave us. God is powerfully and uniquely present to us in these things. In Scripture, we experience the living word of God; we come to understand the history and revelation of God and his plan of salvation for mankind. The Bible is about the truth, not scientific fact. It is the account of God speaking to us both directly and through events. If we read the Bible looking for scientific explanations of things and take everything literally (except for those parts that are supposed to be taken literally), then we miss the point. The Bible has to be read, interpreted, and understood within the historical and cultural context within which it was written. Without a thorough understanding of this, one can use a particular verse or story of the Bible to back up all kinds of ridiculous claims and make all sorts of absurd and mistaken points that have absolutely nothing to do with the purpose for which those verses were originally written. Personal interpretation is very dangerous!

To give one quick example, take the story of Adam and Eve. Do we know with *scientific certainty* that the names of the first two human beings were, in fact, Adam and Eve and that they lived in a garden, took the bad advice of a snake, and ruined their lives and the lives of all who followed after them? The answer is no. And that isn't the point of the story. The point of the story is to relate to us the *truth* that God did create everything; he created everything good including man and woman. Evil did not come from the hand of God, and humanity was made the steward of creation, was given free will, and as a result of disobeying God, brought sin into the world. And that first sin, that first act of disobedience, did *truly* bring chaos, disorder, and evil into the world.

Throughout the Bible, especially in the Old Testament, many stories are used to make a theological statement. Jesus, too, told stories (parables) to relate the truth of a particular matter. Naturally, there are many other instances in Scripture that do tell of actual, factual, historical events of God working in and through certain people, cultures, times, and places to make his presence known and experienced as he brought about his revelation and his plan of salvation.

In the Torah (the first five books of the Bible) we see the reality of God working in and through Moses to deliver his chosen people, the Israelites, out of the bondage of slavery in Egypt and guiding them to the Promised Land. Did everything happen in those stories exactly, with complete and total scientific accuracy, as the author had written? Who knows? Some scientists have come up with various natural explanations for the things that took place. Whether there is a natural explanation for every minute detail or not, it really doesn't matter. God can certainly work through natural means — after all, it's all his creation! The point, the truth, is that *something* happened to bring about this otherwise impossible reality of freedom and deliverance. The truth is that the *something* there was without a doubt the work of God.

In the New Testament, we see many occasions of this *something* happening in which the true manifestation of God is the only possible answer and cause. The biggest occasion of *something* happening is that of the resurrection. We see in Scripture that while Jesus was undergoing his passion and death, all but one of his disciples left him. They turned into spineless cowards who ran in fear and literally went off and locked themselves up in a room to hide out.

Fast forward now to the resurrection. All of a sudden *something* (which we know as the post-resurrection encounters of Jesus and later Pentecost) happened that instantly turned these followers of Jesus from cowards who feared for their lives into men who went out and risked life and limb and who gave their lives for the sake of the gospel. Now, can you really think of anything that could possibly have this kind of an effect on someone other than a true encounter with the Divine? Do you really think some silly magic trick or an elaborate hoax would fill one with that much instant courage and motivation? I don't know about you, but if I were in their shoes, nothing short of a resurrection and a direct influx of the Holy Spirit would have gotten me so fired up.

Yet still, ever since Jesus rose, there are those who doubted and who would not believe, even some of his own disciples initially. And even after Jesus appeared to them, one still would not believe until he was able to put his fingers into the nail holes of his hands. Only then was he convinced. Even though over 500 people experienced the resurrected Jesus before he ascended into heaven (1 Cor 15:6-7), still from that time until today people are filled with doubt and disbelief. Many have tried to come up with all sorts of explanations and conspiracy theories.

In our current time we have things like the best-selling novel *The Da Vinci Code*, which by the way is found in the *fiction* section of bookstores for a reason, and even the proposed "facts" that it is based on are mostly fiction. One of the main ideas presented in the book, which is nothing new, is the notion that Jesus was married to Mary Magdalene. And if he was, great! Marriage was then and is today a great thing! There would have been absolutely no reason to keep it a big hidden secret. But we know from Scripture that this simply was not the case. While dying on the cross, Jesus gave the care of his very own beloved mother to a disciple, an outsider. If Jesus was married or had blood brothers and sisters, he would have obviously given his own mother to them instead of someone who was of no immediate relation to him.

More recently we heard about the declared "lost tomb" of Jesus that was supposed to shake Christianity to its core. And while the vast majority of credible archeologists, scientists, and theologians rolled their eyes, Hollywood rolled in the cash. As we know from studying Christian history, the Tomb of Jesus was never "lost" in the first place. The same tomb that we hear about in Scripture is the same tomb that the first Christians, almost immediately after the resurrection, began to reverence and make pilgrimages to. Later, during the years AD 135-335, a pagan temple was constructed over the tomb in an attempt to blot out this most holy place, but luckily in the year 326 the Emperor Constantine built a basilica at the site to keep it marked as a Holy place for future generations.

But no matter what, conspiracy theories, doubts, and wild suspicions about Jesus, about his Divinity, and about his Church continue to come and go. They always will. And so the question that comes to mind is: Why have people tried so desperately to explain away the resurrection of Jesus? Why do people try so hard to prove he was just a man? Well, because if the resurrection is true, then Jesus is truly the Son of God, and if Jesus is truly the Son of God, then everything he said and taught was indeed the truth. And if that's the case, those who are not living out that truth, those who don't take the teachings of Jesus deadly seriously are in big trouble! It means we really will be held accountable for our sinfulness and our offenses against God. It means that we can no longer justify our godless, faithless ways and atrocities by denying the truth of Christ. And that scares the hell (literally) out of many people.

Meanwhile, for us who do believe, there is no need to worry or entertain such conspiracies and suspicions. As a people of faith, we encounter the risen Christ all the time through his living word, through the very real workings of the Holy Spirit, and through the sacraments. We have no reason to doubt that "*something*."

Another great example of *something* happening is in the conversion of St. Paul. We know that Paul was first known as Saul and was brought up in the strict framework of the Pharisees. While in Jerusalem, Saul took great disliking (to say the least) to the flourishing Christian community there. Saul was present at the stoning of St. Stephen (the first Christian martyr) and made many threats to kill and slaughter those who followed Christ. Saul wanted nothing more than to snuff out the Church and wipe out Christianity forever. He hated Christians with a deep, burning passion!

And so here, a very wise, intelligent, powerful man, who certainly isn't going to be fooled by trickery and crafty deceit, has this incredible experience of the risen Jesus on the road to Damascus

and instantly transforms into a man who, instead of doing everything possible to destroy Christianity, did everything possible to
spread it! *Something* happened! That *something* was again the
power of Christ. Absolutely *nothing* else could have possibly
brought about such a miraculous change, period.

MANIFESTATION OF THE DIVINE OUTSIDE OF SCRIPTURE

THERE ARE ALSO MANY events outside of Scripture in which we
see the true manifestation of the Divine and the handiwork of
Christ. Many of these events have come about recently (and others not so recently) through Jesus' mother, Mary. I'm sure we've all
heard of the different Marian apparitions that have taken place
over the years and the ones that are supposedly going on now.
Self-proclaimed visionaries have claimed to see the Blessed Virgin Mary and to have received messages from her about different
topics of faith and current events. I'll be the first to say that many
of these apparitions are without a doubt unauthentic and are
being used for ulterior motives and hidden agendas. I know this
for a fact. However, there are also apparitions, encounters, and
messages from our Lady that are not hoaxes, that are authentic,
have been approved by the Church, and have brought about truly
miraculous conversions and healings. And for the Catholic
Church to put her stamp of approval on a miracle, you can believe
it is authentic. The Church is the most skeptical of all in regards
to these things, and this is because she wants to be *absolutely* sure
of the authenticity of such happenings.

One such Church-approved and well-known apparition of
Mary is that of her appearance in Mexico — Our Lady of
Guadalupe. As a result of these apparitions and miraculous
events in 1531, millions, that's right, literally millions were converted from pagan religions (complete with the practice of

human sacrifice) to Christ and his Church. The story unfolds like this: One particular day as a simple native Mexican man by the name of (St.) Juan Diego was walking the hill country of Tepayac, he encountered a beautiful lady surrounded by what appeared to be a ball of light as dazzling as the sun.

The lady began to speak to him in his own native language and said, "My dear little son, I love you. I desire you to know who I am. I am the ever-virgin Mary, Mother of the true God who gives life and maintains its existence. He created all things. He is in all places. He is Lord of Heaven and Earth. I desire a church in this place where your people may experience my compassion. All those who sincerely ask my help in their work and in their sorrows will know my Mother's Heart in this place. Here I will see their tears; I will console them and they will be at peace. So run now to Tenochtitlan and tell the Bishop all that you have seen and heard."

And so with this, Juan rushed to see the Bishop and tell him what had just happened. The Bishop didn't exactly buy Juan's story, and so Juan returned to the hill where he encountered Mary to ask her to send someone else whose words perhaps might carry a little more weight. Our Lady instead told him, "My little son, there are many I could send. But you are the one I have chosen." She then instructed him to go back the next day and try again with the request.

After hours of waiting, the Bishop finally once again agreed to see Juan and after hearing his fantastically dubious story for the second time, he asked Juan to see if our Lady would provide some kind of sign or proof that this message was authentic. Juan returned to the hill once more and relayed the Bishop's message to Mary who was waiting for him there, and she responded, "Very well, my son. Return here tomorrow and you can take to the Bishop the sign he has requested. Then he will believe you. He will no longer doubt you or be suspicious of you. And know, my son, that I shall reward your solicitude, effort, and fatigue on my behalf. Go now, and tomorrow I shall await you here."

On the following day, however, Juan was not able to return to the hill because his uncle had become seriously ill. Two days later, with his uncle on the verge of death, Juan went in search of a priest. As he passed the hill of Tepayac in a frantic rush, he found Mary waiting for him. She said, "Do not be distressed, my littlest son. Am I not here with you who am your Mother? Are you not under my shadow and protection? Your uncle will not die at this time. There is no reason for you to engage a priest, for his health is restored at this moment. He is quite well. Go to the top of the hill and cut the flowers that are growing there. Bring them then to me."

Even though it was freezing cold on the hillside, Juan did as Mary asked and went to the top of the hill where he found a full bloom of Castilian roses. Removing his tilma (a poncho-like cape made of cactus fiber), he cut the roses and carried them back to Mary. Upon his arrival, Our Lady told him, "My little son, this is the sign I am sending to the Bishop. Tell him that with this sign I request his greatest efforts to complete the church I desire in this place. Show these flowers to no one else but the Bishop. You are my trusted ambassador. This time the Bishop will believe all you tell him."

Juan again went to the Bishop, related his message and opened his tilma to present the flowers. Immediately the Bishop and his advisors who were present fell to their knees, not so much because of the miraculous out-of-season flowers, but because of a beautiful image of Mary, exactly as Juan described her, which was now present on the tilma.

The next day, after presenting the tilma at the Cathedral, Juan took the Bishop to the location where Mary had first appeared to him. He then went home to his village where he discovered that his uncle was completely cured.

Juan's uncle recalled how he had met a lady surrounded by a glowing light who told him that she had sent his nephew to Tenochtitlan with a picture of herself. She said to him, "Call me and call my image Santa Maria de Guadalupe."

But the story doesn't end there. As a result of these events, within six years of this apparition, six million Aztecs had converted to Catholicism. The tilma itself is fascinating to say the least and depicts Mary as the "God-bearer," pregnant with her Divine Son. Every little detail of the image has significance and meaning. There is way too much information to go into here so I simply recommend to the reader to study further this beautiful and sacred image.

The tilma has been subjected to a multitude of environmental hazards over the years. It's been exposed to such things as smoke from fires and candles, and water from floods and heavy rains. To top it all off, the tilma miraculously survived an explosion from a bomb in 1921 that was planted by anticlerical forces. A cast-iron cross that was next to the tilma was severely damaged, as was the nearby marble altar, but the tilma remained free from even the slightest blemish.

Over the years, the tilma has been studied by scientists using infrared photography, digital enhancement, and the like, and they have concluded that the method in which the image was created is unknown. There are many other intriguing scientific findings that give witness to the truly miraculous nature of this image and the tilma that bears it. Of course, like with anything else that bears the title "miraculous," there are scientists who desperately try to debunk these findings.

The bottom line is that here again, *something* happened to St. Juan Diego. *Something* happened to change the mind and heart of a very skeptical Bishop and to cure Juan's uncle. *Something* happened to convert millions of people from a pagan religion that demanded the human blood of their own innocent people, to faith in Jesus Christ. *Something* happened to keep the tilma from being blown to bits by a bomb and to keep it perfectly preserved for hundreds of years so that great multitudes of pilgrims can see it still today. That *something* is ultimately the work of God.

GOD IN THE SACRAMENTS

So, WHILE WE SEE the true manifestation and workings of God in his word and in the many events of our lives and in our world, one of the most prominent ways that God leaves his sign and truly enters into our lives (through his Church) is by means of the sacraments he gave us.

The sacraments are not just symbols or mere reenactments of God's interaction with humanity. They are true, supernatural experiences of God in which he draws us nearer and bestows his grace upon us. And grace is not just a pleasant, comforting idea about something that helps us be good or makes us feel nice. Grace is a real and active participation in the life of God. Grace is very genuine and very powerful! It is a true elixir for the soul! The more of it we have, the more able we become to reject the glamour of evil, stay free from the enslaving bondage of sin, and become more Christ-like. But, like any good medicine, if we don't take it, it won't do a thing for us.

The Church teaches us that,

Grace is *favor*, the *free and undeserved* help that God gives us to respond to his call to become children of God, adoptive sons and daughters, and partakers of the divine nature and of eternal life. (CCC 1996)

The grace that we receive in the sacraments, though, is not magic. You'll hear me say this over and over throughout this book. We have to work in cooperation with the power of grace. If we do this, we experience the real, potent, transforming dynamism of it.

When one is working in cooperation with grace, he or she will experience things like the sudden strength to avoid a particular sin or temptation that he or she has been struggling with, that in the past he or she has been virtually helpless to overcome. While working in cooperation with grace, one will have a new-found desire to simply do the right thing, the Christ-like thing, to exercise charity and virtue with great fervor. Grace begets a desire for genuine holiness of life.

When one is not working in cooperation with grace, the life and nourishment that is offered and given in the sacraments is not experienced to the fullest. For example, if a child is baptized and then is never brought to church, never taught the faith, and never included in the active life of the Christian community, then that child will most likely not experience to the fullest the true potential of the grace given in Baptism. If a couple receives the sacrament of Matrimony and then essentially kicks God and the Church out of their married life, they will most likely not experience the life-giving, unifying, sanctifying grace that God has given them in that sacrament. If one goes to the sacrament of Reconciliation, confesses one's sins, but does not have a contrite heart or firm purpose of amendment to go forth and truly strive to "sin no more," then the grace of that sacrament will not have the effect that it could and should.

While there are things that we do by means of our actions and intentions that keep us from cooperating with sacramental grace, there are also a number of things that have to be present in order for a sacrament to be valid. First of all, the person administering the sacrament must be qualified to do so, which in most cases is a validly ordained priest or deacon. There are some exceptions, such as emergency Baptism, in which anyone can baptize validly. Additionally, in the case of Matrimony the husband and wife actually administer the sacrament to each other, but a priest or deacon must witness it.

It is important to keep in mind also that the effect of a sacrament comes *ex opere operato* (by the very fact of being administered) and is not dependent upon the personal holiness of the person administering it. What this means is that if (God forbid) an unrepentant, sinful, disgraceful priest has just heard your confession and given you absolution, as long as he performed the sacrament correctly, the grace of the sacrament is still valid. Thankfully, God gives us his grace and enters into our lives through the sacraments despite the failings of his ministers. No one could ever be holy enough and good enough to be worthy of such a responsibility and task. As one of my seminary professors used to say, "The life-giving grace of God comes out the same whether the faucet is gold-plated or is old and tarnished."

Secondly, for a sacrament to be valid, the minister must use the proper form (prescribed words) along with the proper actions, while using the proper substance (water, oil, bread, wine, and so on). I heard a story once of a hippie-priest back in the '70s who decided to celebrate Mass dressed up like a clown and used pizza and grape soda instead of the prescribed bread and wine for the Eucharist. Needless to say, it was not a valid Mass.

Thirdly, the minister of the sacrament must have the proper intention for the sacrament: to do what the Church, and ultimately Christ, intended the sacrament for. A priest cannot "do his own thing" with the sacraments. They are not his, or anybody else's, to tamper with. They belong to Jesus and his Church, which he established to be under the leadership of the successor of St. Peter and the apostles.

In Scripture, we see that Jesus often used things like water, wine, bread, oil, and so forth as mediums through which he performed miracles. We use these same mediums as the physical signs of the sacraments. But again, the sacraments are not just physical, symbolic signs. It is through these natural elements that God manifests his supernatural presence. The seven sacraments of the Church, which were instituted by Christ, are: Baptism, Reconciliation, Eucharist, Confirmation, Matrimony, Holy Orders, and Anointing of the Sick. Though the practices and disciplines in which the sacraments are distributed, performed, and received have changed over the years, their sacred reality has remained rooted in the actions and teachings of Christ Jesus.

The sacraments each have particular challenges for us in regard to preparing for them, receiving them, and living them out in an ongoing fashion. They make up the framework and foundation of our lives as Catholics. They constitute a good portion of the meat and potatoes of our faith and of our lives as followers of Jesus Christ and members of his Church. They are things that we should not take lightly. We should have a thorough understanding of them and have a strong desire to implement them to their greatest potential in our lives throughout our spiritual and earthly journey.

That being said, the remainder of this book (for the most part) does just that: takes a good look at the beauty, the power, the transforming reality, the presence, and the love of God, who enters into our lives in such a dynamic and real way by means of these great gifts of his sacraments. It also looks at issues such as the preparation for the sacraments, who receives them and why, and other related areas that often interest Catholics as well as some of the hot-button issues that come up with some of them.

CHAPTER 3

COME TO THE WATER

COME ALONG WITH ME. Watch your step, it's a bit muddy through this part. Here we are . . . see that log over there . . . the one with the green fuzzy moss on the end, with the bark peeling away . . . that's the one. Have a seat. Be still for a second. Don't make any fast motions now. Shhhhhhhh.

Did you hear that? A fish flopped in the water over there . . . he must be feeding on those minnows . . . just like these . . . see 'em here in the shallows hiding behind those dark rocks? They really blend in, don't they? Look at those beavers over there in the slough. Check out all those trees they cut down to build their den. Those things can really chop some wood! They're just working away over there, busy as . . . well . . . beavers! Looks like fun.

That breeze sure feels nice, eh? Wait a minute . . . is that . . . sure enough . . . look down the line over there, just beyond that brush on the bank . . . it's a big mama deer and her two fawns. They're just munching away over there. I'll bet they came down to get a drink of water to wash down all those acorns. I'll tell you, there's nothing quite as soothing as the sound of the water running over and through these rocks. The deer like it, too. Aahhh . . . I could listen to that all day!

Hey, look at that! A flock of turkeys just flew across the water way down at the bend! There they go, up and over the next ridge. It really is astounding how those big, huge birds can fly like that.

They just jump up, spread those monstrous wings, and flap and glide through the air like great, black dragons!

Watch this . . . see that slick, brown rock right there, this one . . . right here on the edge of the water? Look what's hiding under it in the little cracks and crevices . . . see here . . . all kinds of little aquatic insects and such. See this one? That's a scud . . . trout love 'em!

I'll bet the bottom seam of that gravel bar over there is loaded with crawdads. No wonder all those big fish are in the hole below that riffle. Wow! Check out the snake in that tree . . . see it? The fallen maple tree . . . right there. And look at those two big turtles on the stump trying to get some sun. I guess it can get kind of chilly with that big, cold shell on your back all day. They seem to be pretty content, though.

There it is again! Man, that is a big fish feeding up there! It sounds like a brick hitting the water when he jumps out and flops around like that. Whoa! Now that is neat! Look at the Great Blue Heron gliding across the water down there. It's incredible how such a monstrous bird can be so graceful and quiet. She looks like a pterodactyl from the days of the dinosaurs! She's looking for a good place to fish, no doubt. After all, they didn't get the nickname, "the fisherman's friend" for nothing, you know. Yep. She landed. Watch how she'll stalk ever so slowly up to that little eddy there, and then with lightning speed, fire that long, spear-like beak down to catch a fish. Amazing!

The wind is picking up a bit, eh? Listen to those trees squeaking and grinding as they rustle back in the woods there. Sounds like they're talking to each other. I wonder what they're saying? You know, many of these trees have been here long before you or I were born. Think of all they've witnessed over the decades. They've listened to the desperate pleas and the peaceful prayers of many who have come and gone. They just keep on growing, perilously reaching up to heaven. Can't blame 'em for that, that's where I want to go.

Look up there, up in the sky! See those geese overhead? I wonder where they are going. Listen to that . . . "honk, honk, honk, honk" . . . there must be a dozen or more. I wish I could go with them; I'd like to get away for awhile. How do those things navigate so well? Just amazing! Ha-ha . . . see that? That pair of otters over there in those exposed tree roots. They're just slipping and sliding along. Probably looking to catch that big fish who's up there making all that commotion. I reckon fish for breakfast wouldn't be too bad?

Just think about it for a minute . . . where did this batch of water come from? Where is it going? It just keeps on flowing and tumbling, rolling on down the line. Roll, roll, roll, constantly changing, transforming, and giving life to everything around here. This river is the lifeline, the main artery that runs through the heart of this land. Every creature that walks and crawls, runs and swims, slithers and flies, and talks like you and me depends on this river and on this water. They come here to be refreshed, nourished, renewed, cleansed, and calmed. Without it, we'd all just dry up and fade away. You know, I wish I could stay right here with you forever.

Whoops . . . looks like some clouds are moving in. Sure enough . . . did you feel that rain drop? There's another one, and another one. Yep, it's raining all right, get ready . . . here it comes. But you know what? I really don't mind; let's stay right here. It's picking up now . . . just be still for awhile and listen . . . Aahhhhhh!

I could listen to that for all eternity! It really does cleanse one's soul and wash the troubles away. I feel born again every time the rain comes. I feel purified, as if God is washing me clean like a little baby getting his first bath. You know, in the midst of all this aquatic clamor, there is a peace and stillness that is truly euphoric to enter into.

The rain genuinely has a siren song about it if you listen carefully. It'll draw you in to a divine dimension. At this moment nothing else matters. There is nowhere to go and nothing to be done. There is simply one drop, then another, and another. Each drop is exclusively individual, yet all together, united as one rain, their sound becomes symphonic as it blankets us in this sacred solitude. I kind of feel like a kid hiding out in my cardboard box fortress. Remember that? Remember that feeling of comfort and peace, of being in a dwelling place uniquely your own? That's how I feel right now. That's how I feel as a spiritual being, a physical being, a human being, dwelling here in this body of mine and in this place of life.

I know, you think I'm a bit weird, but I can't help it. Being here at the river really does something to me. Water = life. It's one of the main ingredients God uses to make everything, including us. But of course water isn't always so nice. Just as it can foster and support life, it can also bring about death and destruction. Remember the flood that came through here back in '93? Unbelievable!

This entire area was an underwater wasteland! Heck, that water was halfway up the ridge over there. See that scour mark across the top? Did you notice that pile of gigantic dead trees when we came down this path? Those were all uprooted and bulldozed over by the raging waters. Remember that lush clover field back the way, there? That entire thing was a burned out, lifeless, sand pit for some time after the flood came through. You know those club houses and boat docks we saw earlier? They were all completely demolished and reduced to a pile of rubble after that summer. Most of the wood from those houses is probably down in the Gulf of Mexico somewhere now.

Boy, that was something else! How many people lost their lives in that one? How many neighborhoods around these parts were wiped out? I can't recall the exact number either, but it was lots! All those old, historic buildings are gone. So many poor folks lost everything in just a matter or days: their homes, their cars, their businesses, their farms and livestock . . . all gone. I'd never seen so much rain as that summer. Every day, all day for months, it seemed like . . . rain, rain, rain, rain, and rain some more. I thought we were going to have to build an ark!

Remember when the levee broke? Power lines were knocked out, huge propane tanks were bobbing along like floating time bombs, and there was just mass chaos everywhere! This river literally turned into an ocean of death! You couldn't see where it ended. There was no hope in sight. We spent many days and nights throwing sand bags and helping people get moved out before their homes went under. That's a summer I'll never forget! Hopefully we won't see something like that again for a long, long time!

But even after those seemingly horrific acts of destruction, new life again slowly emerged. When the flood waters subsided, the ground was recharged with vital nutrients; new channels and underwater structures were created. Mother Earth reclaimed her wandering children and began a new ecological portrait with a blank canvas and a palate of recycled colors and hues.

THE TRANSFORMING POWER OF WATER
AND THE SACRAMENT OF BAPTISM

WATER BRINGS LIFE, water brings death, water brings constant transformation. It can transform from rain, to ice, to snow. It can change from a peaceful shower to a psychotic, bloodthirsty, torrential downpour. It can sustain life, or it can blast it into oblivion in one, mad rush. Water can magnetically draw to itself all of creation, or it can choke and drown the breath out of all the living. Water can sicken, and water can heal.

With water being such a multifaceted element, it's really no wonder that it is the primary sign used during the sacrament of Baptism. The blessing of the water during the Rite of Baptism gives witness to this and sums it up well:

> Father, you give us grace through sacramental signs, which reminds us of the wonders of your unseen power. In baptism we use your gift of water, which you have made as a rich symbol of the grace you give us in this sacrament. At the very dawn of creation, your Spirit breathed on the waters, making them the wellspring of all holiness. The waters of the great flood you made a sign of the waters' power that make an end of sin and a new beginning of goodness. Through the waters of the Red Sea you led Israel out of slavery to be an image of God's holy people, set free from sin by baptism. In the waters of the Jordan, your son was baptized by John and anointed with the Spirit. Your Son willed that water and blood should flow from him as he hung upon the cross. After his resurrection, he told his disciples: "Go out and teach all nations, baptizing them in the name of the Father, and of the Son, and of the Holy Spirit." Father, look now with love upon your Church, and unseal for her the fountain of baptism. By the power of the Spirit, give to the water of this font the grace of your Son. You create man in your own likeness: cleanse him from sin in a new birth to innocence by water and the Spirit.[1]

This beautiful prayer makes the point well concerning the transforming power of water and how God has used it throughout salvation history. It is important to recognize that every living creature on earth experiences transformation throughout life. For us as human beings, those changes and transformations are often marked by significant events in our lives. No matter how old or how young we are, all of us can think of things we've experienced that have significantly changed us and transformed us in some way, either in a good way or bad way.

Learning to walk significantly changes our lives, as does learning to talk. Learning to drive, graduating from school, moving away from home, getting a job, and becoming financially independent are all things that transform us. Getting married, becoming a parent, or getting ordained are all things that bring many changes. All of these are defining moments for us. They are things we never forget. They are events that forever change who we are.

One of the most important, transforming events that we experience — most of us probably don't remember and often don't even realize the effect it has had on us — is our baptism. Baptism is one of the sacraments that leaves a permanent mark on our souls. It forever changes and transforms who and what we are in the eyes of God. It permanently alters the very nature of our being. Every time we come into church and place our hands in the holy water and make the Sign of the Cross, we (should) remind ourselves of our baptism and the reality that we are children of God.

Baptism is where it all begins for us as Catholics. It is the starting point of our spiritual journey. By means of our baptism we are set free from the shackles of sin and death. The stain of original sin is washed away and we are purified and bathed with God's saving grace. We are reborn as God's adopted sons and daughters. The waters of Baptism signify our sharing in Jesus' death and resurrection and our becoming new creatures in Christ. Now, all this sounds great of course, but so often we don't fully realize what this means and the implications it has for us. This being the case, I'd like to take you on another guided journey; we'll go step by step through the sacrament of Baptism. But first, let's take a look at what Scripture and Sacred Tradition have to say on the matter.

In the Acts of the Apostles, we hear about the nature of Baptism. St. Peter proclaims, "Repent, and be baptized every one of you in the name of Jesus Christ for the forgiveness of your sins; and you shall receive the gift of the Holy Spirit" (Acts 2:38). It is important to point out that St. Peter also included children in his message, as he went on to say, "For the promise is to you and to your children and to all that are far off, every one whom the Lord our God calls to him" (2:39). Later on, in Chapter 22, we hear, "Rise and be baptized, and wash away your sins, calling on his name" (v. 22). In 1 Peter 3:21, we hear a further distinction: "Baptism, which now saves you, is not a removal of dirt from the body but an appeal to God for a clear conscience, through the resurrection of Jesus Christ."

St. Paul has a thing or two to say about Baptism as well. In Romans 6:3-4, we hear, "Do you not know that all of us who have been baptized into Christ Jesus were baptized into his death? We were buried therefore with him by baptism into death, so that as Christ was raised from the dead by the glory of the Father, we too might walk in newness of life."

In Colossians 2:11-13, St. Paul states, "In him you were also circumcised with a circumcision not administered by hand, by stripping off the carnal body, with the circumcision of Christ. You were buried with him in baptism, in which you were also raised with him through faith in the power of God, who raised him from the dead. And even when you were dead in transgressions and the uncircumcision of your flesh, he brought you to life along with him, having forgiven us all our transgressions."

In this passage from Colossians, St. Paul makes it known that for the Christian, Baptism has replaced circumcision. Under the Jewish law of the Old Testament, infants were circumcised as a part of their ritualized entrance into the Jewish faith. It was not all that common for adults to convert to Judaism, but if they did, they too would have to undergo circumcision along with being trained in the ways of the faith. And so, the parallels remained the same for Christians; the child of a Christian family would be baptized and then brought up in the faith by his or her parents and adults who converted to the faith would be trained, educated, and then baptized as well. Today we do this through the Rite of Christian Initiation for Adults (RCIA) program.

The practice of baptizing infants and children along with adults goes back to the days of the very first Christians, and there is indication of this in Scripture as well. We hear in the Acts of the Apostles of individuals and their entire households (including children) being baptized. If there were exceptions to this practice, they would have been indicated. But still, infant baptism has remained an area of concern for some non-Catholics and Catholics alike. Some say, "Shouldn't we wait for a child to grow up and then make his/her own decision to be baptized and become a Christian?" Along those same lines, we could ask such questions as, "Should we wait for a child to grow up before we teach him/her a certain language? After all, he or she might not like English."

Children obviously do not choose things such as who their parents are going to be, what country they are going to live in, where they are going to go to school, what they are going to eat in order to grow up healthy and strong. Parents make these decisions with the child's best interest in mind. They want what is best for their children and what will be of the most value for them as they mature and grow into adolescence and eventually adulthood. In a similar manner, bringing a child into God's family and raising him or her in the ways of the faith of Jesus Christ is simply a good thing to do. Just as a mother would not withhold milk from her baby, so too we should not withhold the grace of God from a child either. As Jesus himself said, "Let the little children come to me, and do not hinder them; for to such belongs the kingdom of God" (Mt 19:14).

When we look at the life of Jesus, we see that as an infant he was taken by Joseph and Mary to the Temple to be consecrated to the Lord in accordance with Jewish law. It is on this occasion that we hear those beautiful words of Simeon, who waited all his life for the moment when he would lay his eyes on the messiah: "Lord, now lettest thou thy servant depart in peace, according to thy word; for mine eyes have seen thy salvation which thou hast prepared in the presence of all peoples, a light for revelation to the Gentiles, and for glory to thy people Israel" (Lk 2:29-32). We also hear his words to Mary, describing the sorrow she will experience, "Behold, this child is set for the fall and rising of many in Israel, and for a sign that is spoken against (and a sword will pierce through your own soul also), that thoughts out of many hearts may be revealed" (Lk 2:34-35).

It was not until Jesus was an adult, at the beginning of his public ministry, that he was baptized; this was for a specific reason. In Scripture, we hear how Jesus approached John to be baptized and how unworthy and hesitant John was to do this, recognizing that Jesus should baptize him instead. But there was a reason Jesus came to John to be baptized. When we were baptized, we came to the water to be set free of original sin and to be reborn into a life of grace, but when Jesus came to the water to be baptized, *it was not the water that transformed him; it was he who transformed the water.* It was Jesus who purified the waters and consecrated them for us and for all people, so that our sinful nature may be washed away and the Holy Spirit may come to dwell in our lives.

THE RITE OF BAPTISM

THE ACTUAL RITE OF BAPTISM is a beautiful, rich, fascinating, and profoundly sacred experience. As with most everything else in our Catholic faith, though, we must have a good understanding and a thorough appreciation of what is actually taking place within both the tangible and the spiritual dimensions to fully enter into the magnificence of it all. Most parishes require the parents of the child to be baptized to attend a class in which they are educated and informed (to varying degrees) about what is involved in the ritual, what its implications are, and what will take place during the actual administration and reception of the sacrament. Adults preparing for Baptism also go through all of this necessary information as a part of their RCIA program. In the next few pages, I go step by step through the sacrament of Baptism. I use the Rite for the Baptism of Children for our example and guide, but most of the procedure is very similar for adults who are to be baptized as well.

Ideally, the Rite of Baptism should begin at the entrance of the Church, or at least in an area located away from the baptistry, that is, the area containing the baptismal font . . . you know . . . the big fancy bowl of water. Even this simple gesture has meaning and significance. After the first part of the ceremony, the family and priest then enter into the Church and process to the area of the baptismal font. This is done to signify the reality that this child is literally entering into the Church as well, not just the building, but the family of God, the Body of Christ. This simple action reflects the reality that this child is beginning her spiritual journey, that he is entering into a new

life of grace as God's son or daughter. It also should be a reminder to the parents and godparents that they, too, are taking
on a new responsibility, as they will be committing to raise this
child in accordance with the faith that he or she is about to be
baptized into.

To go back to square one, as the family gathers with the
priest at the beginning of the rite, the priest asks the simple question of the parents, "What name have you given your child?"[2]
The parents then naturally respond by stating the child's name.
It has long been the tradition for Catholics to give their child a
Christian name, such as that of a saint. In doing so, the child
then has his or her own patron saint and will hopefully look to
that saint for guidance, intercession, and inspiration throughout
his or her life.

After stating the child's name, the priest asks, "What do you
ask of God's Church for ... (name)?"[3] The proper response here
is simply, "Baptism." Now, here comes the important part: the
priest then says to the parents, "You have asked to have your child
baptized. In doing so, you are accepting the responsibility of training him/her in the practice of the faith. It will be your duty to
bring him/her up to keep God's commandments as Christ taught
us, by loving God and our neighbor. Do you clearly understand
what you are undertaking?"[4] He also asks the godparents, "Are
you ready to help the parents of this child in their duty as Christian parents?"[5] The obvious responses to these questions are, "We
do" and "We are." What I'm about to say next is going to sound
a bit shocking to some, and might not seem very nice perhaps, but
the cold, hard truth is that this response of "We do" is, in way too
many cases, simply a bold-faced lie.

As any priest will tell you, out of the hundreds of children
we baptize, we may never see many of them in church with their
parents again, except for maybe Christmas and Easter. After the

nice baptismal ceremony is over and all the cute pictures are taken (and they really are cute ... I'm not being facetious), that child and his or her parents rarely ever step foot in Church again. Even though many of these same parents send their child to a Catholic school, they still do not back up in the home what they *promised* and *committed* to do at their child's baptism. That is, to be the first and best teachers of their child in the ways of the faith, to truly take responsibility for their child's spiritual development, to back up in the home what their child is learning in their Catholic school or Parish School of Religion program. Without that support system at home, Catholic education is a waste of time and money, and more importantly, the grace given at Baptism is never activated.

It is with great disgust and true sadness that I tell you, upon more than one occasion, I have had parents actually smirk and snicker while proclaiming their, "We do." On one particular occasion, the parents were not only completely aloof to what they were committing to in the presence of God, but they were so concerned with the video production and photography of their baby's baptism that they even cut me off right in the middle of the ritual to give directions to their personal camera crew! It was the only time I ever lost my temper (and rightly so) while administering the sacraments. Needless to say, this pathetic, shallow display and behavior is *not* acting in cooperation with the sacrament of Baptism. The sacraments are not for our entertainment, they are in place for our salvation.

All right ... enough of my ranting (though it needs to be heard). Let's get back to the ritual. After the parents accept their responsibility (and many of them truly do, thank God), the priest welcomes the child into the Christian community by tracing the Sign of the Cross on the child's forehead and invites the parents and godparents to do the same. The family and the priest then process to a part of the church that is suitable for the celebration of the word of God. During this phase of the ritual, a reading from Scripture will take place followed by a short homily concerning the nature of baptism, the responsibility it carries, and things of that sort.

After reflecting on Scripture for a bit, intercessory prayers, or the "Prayer of the Faithful," will be recited. Here, those present pray for God's blessing on the child to be baptized, on the parents and godparents, and that all in attendance may live in accordance with the grace they received at their baptism. These prayers are concluded with a litany of the saints at which time we call upon the aid and prayers of those holy men and women who have gone before us and are now dwelling in God's omnipotent presence in heaven.

The next step in the Rite of Baptism is the prayer of exorcism and anointing. Here we ask God to free this child from original sin and to keep him or her free from the evil of Satan. At this point many ask, "What exactly is original sin?" Original sin is our inherited (from Adam and Eve, our first parents) tendency to disobey God. It is our seemingly natural gravitation to be rebellious against God and to stray from him. It is our inclination toward the "glamour of evil," as we say. By means of Baptism we become truly free. We now have a choice; we can say "no" to sin and evil instead of being enslaved by it and mastered by it. By means of Baptism we open the floodgates of God's massive outpouring of grace, which is what genuinely gives us true freedom.

Obviously, we who are baptized still sin. We all know people who are baptized who have done horrible things and committed unspeakable atrocities. It is important to keep in mind that baptism does not take away our free will. God gave us free will that we may love him and others freely, without being forced. After all, we can't *make* someone love us. But by means of our free will, we can still reject God if we wish. We can still put the shackles of sin back if we wish. We can still even send ourselves to hell if we wish, but by means of Baptism, we have the freedom to choose to *not* do those things. The choice is still ours. We can put up roadblocks and place many obstacles in the way of God's saving grace if we want, and that is exactly what we do so often. But again, it doesn't have to be that way, because of our baptism.

After the prayer of exorcism, the child is then anointed on the chest with the oil of *catechumens* (meaning one who is preparing to become a Christian). The use of holy oil and the practice of blessing one with it go back to ancient times and were also used during the initiation of the first Christians. Oil was (and still is for that matter) used for things such as healing and strengthening. Thus, this anointing the child with oil signifies the child being strengthened by Christ so that he or she may grow up to be strong in body, mind, and spirit to fight the good fight and reject sin and evil. This reality is validated as the priest then proclaims, "May you have strength in the power of Christ our Savior, who lives and reigns for ever."[6]

At this point, the family and the priest gather at the font for the actual baptism. This part of the ritual begins with the prayer of blessing and invocation over the water that I referred to a few pages back. After the water has been blessed, the priest reminds the parents, "You have come here to present this child for baptism. By water and the Holy Spirit he/she is to receive the gift of new life from God, who is love. On your part, you must make it your constant care to bring him/her up in the practices of the faith. See that the divine life which God gives him/her is kept safe from the poison of sin, to grow always stronger in his/her heart."[7] Then, the priest asks the parents and godparents to profess their faith by answering a series of questions.

After the family has professed their faith and expressed their commitment to raise their child in the faith, the child is baptized with water "in the name of the Father, the Son, and the Holy Spirit." This basic formula of being baptized with water in the name of the Holy Trinity is the basis for any valid baptism, including those of other Christian denominations. We do not re-baptize someone of another Christian denomination if they are converting to Catholicism as long as they were validly baptized in the manner prescribed.

The actual baptism can be done either by pouring water over the head of the person or by complete immersion in the water. Here is where that transforming power of water comes into play. Being completely immersed into water is a profound and telling witness to the reality of dying and being born again. As one goes down into the water, the old self, dominated by original sin, dies. As one rises up out of the water, he or she shares in the resurrection of Christ. As St. Paul tells us in Romans 6:3-4, which we looked at earlier, "Do you not know that all of us who have been baptized into Christ Jesus were baptized into his death? We were buried therefore with him by baptism into death, so that as Christ was raised from the dead by the glory of the Father, we too might walk in newness of life." As the individual then rises up out of the water, it is a rising up to a new life of grace. At this point, the nature of who and what the person is in the eyes of God is permanently changed; he or she has become a child of God and a member of his family, the Church. The individual has been made a new creation in Christ! Of course, the same thing happens when water is simply poured over the head, but the reality of what is taking place isn't communicated quite as vividly as full body immersion baptisms. The practice of one method or the other simply depends on what a particular Church facility is able to accommodate.

After the actual baptizing is complete, the child or adult will then be anointed with the oil of Chrism. Chrism is another of the three Holy oils used in Catholicism. It is a mixture of pure olive oil and balsam. It has a wonderful fragrance, which makes it quite distinct from the other two oils (oil of catechumens and oil of the sick). Chrism also has its origins in ancient days and is still used today to consecrate something or someone to God. It is used during the sacraments of Confirmation and Holy Orders and is also used during the consecration of sacred things such as church, altar, chalice, and the like.

Before the priest anoints the newly baptized with the oil of Chrism on the crown of the head, he speaks a very important message: "God, the Father of our Lord Jesus Christ, has freed you from sin, given you new birth by water and the Holy Spirit, and welcomes you into his holy people. He now anoints you with the Chrism of salvation. As Christ was anointed Priest, Prophet, and King, so may you live always as a member of his body, sharing everlasting life."[8]

OUR BAPTISMAL VOCATION

IT IS AT THIS POINT that we have all been given our basic mission in life. Here is where our baptismal vocation and calling is laid before us. All of us, by means of the sacrament of Baptism, are called to share in the life of Jesus as "priest, prophet, and king." This three-fold mission does require a more thorough explanation, of course. I wouldn't leave you hanging on that one!

For starters, we are called to share in the life and mission of Jesus as priest. The priesthood that we all share in is called the *priesthood of the faithful.* This is different from the ordained, sacramental priesthood (I'll cover that in a later chapter). A priest of any religion becomes a priest for one specific reason: to offer a sacrifice. That is the nature and primary function of a priest. Now obviously, we ordained priests are involved in all kinds of different things, and we have a multitude of responsibilities and tasks to fulfill every week, but the main reason we exist is to offer the sacrifice of the Mass, to make Jesus substantially present to his people and to his Church. Everything else we do draws its meaning and purpose from the Eucharistic sacrifice.

So, while the ordained priest offers what we call the *cultic* sacrifice (the sacrifice of the Mass), all of us as a part of the priesthood of the faithful offer to God the *spiritual sacrifices* of our lives. As we go though life, we offer to God the joys and blessings that we experience as a sacrifice of praise and thanksgiving. When we find ourselves in difficult times, beat down with pain and misery, we offer to God the sacrifice of our suffering. No matter what is going on in our lives, we are called to include God by offering it to him. We can do this at anytime by means of simply praying to God and offering him the good, the bad, and the ugly of our daily experiences.

But at Mass we should consciously place those spiritual sacrifices on the altar to be offered up to the Father, along with his Son, in the Eucharistic sacrifice of the Mass. This is another reason it's so important to get to Mass early and spend time in prayer, reviewing your life and truly entering into that sacred encounter. Take your priesthood seriously! By consciously offering up those spiritual sacrifices, we can do an abundance of good for our souls and the souls of countless others.

Secondly, we share in the mission of Christ as prophet. A prophet is one who proclaims something. Although Jesus was the fulfillment of all the Old Testament prophesy and that of John the Baptist, it is Jesus himself who proclaimed the good news of the gospel. It is Jesus, the Son of God, who taught and revealed to us who God is, what God is like, what the fulfillment of his plan is for us and how much God loves us. We, too, are called to proclaim the good news of the Gospel, and there are lots of different ways to do that. Not many of us will take to the streets or set up a pulpit in the break room at work and boldly teach and preach the message of Christ with fiery enthusiasm and unstoppable vigor. Not many of us will leave everything behind and head off to a mysterious, foreign land to proclaim the gospel to the ears of those who have never heard it — although perhaps some of us *will* do those things.

Along those same lines, I'm sure we all know people who constantly preach to us, either in our families, at work, or somewhere else. We all know those folks we dub as "religious fanatics," who shove the good news down our throats whether we like it or not! There are more than a few stouthearted individuals who will thump you over the head with the Bible so hard that you won't be able to see straight for days! Indeed, some of us might be called to be rather aggressive in our shared mission as prophet, but we have to also exercise the virtues of prudence and patience. When we violently shove things down people's throats, the only result is that they will choke to death or throw it right back up, and we all know that isn't pretty!

That being said, though, it is important to be willing and proactive in sharing our faith with others, to not be afraid of or embarrassed by practicing our faith. There is no reason to apologize for who and what we are as Catholics. Sure, there a lot of Catholics (priests and bishops included) who have done things to publicly shame us all. That's the reason it's vitally important to get out there and be a good example, to be a living witness of what we are truly called to be as followers of Christ and members of his Church.

The most potent and influential method of fulfilling our vocation as prophet and proclaiming the gospel message is by means of the example we set. Actions do often speak much, much louder than words. Our actions can speak with the same skull-splitting volume of one of those legendary rock and roll performances by (the now) deaf and dumb band of your choice!

When we make it a point to *not* participate in the sinful activities of our peers or coworkers, we send a powerful message. When we make it a point to keep ourselves in constant check with Christ-like thoughts, words, and deeds, with that same aforementioned volume, we exercize our prophetic ministry. When we make a stand for what we know is right and take action or speak out on an important matter, we proclaim the good news. There are lots and lots of opportunities each and every day to either be a witness for Christ or to cast aside our Christian dignity, which we were given at Baptism, and plunge ourselves headlong, like a herd of fat-faced, half-blind feral hogs, into the swill-ridden, demon-infested mud pit of putrid, stench-filled filth of sin that so much of our culture revels in and slops up day in and day out . . . nasty!

Thirdly, we are called to share in the mission of Christ as King. Now that sounds great, right!? A king!? Yeah! Who wouldn't want to be a king? After all, kings are rich and mighty, they have an abundance of wealth, they call the shots on everything, they have people serving them and attending to their every whim. Well, sorry folks, but that's not the kind of a king Jesus was (while he was here on earth). The only crown he ever wore was a crown of thorns. The only seat of distinction Jesus was ever given was on the back of a donkey. The robe he wore was not made of priceless, extravagant linen of a noble weave. His robe was fairly simple, and it was not worn with valor, but was instead ripped off his blood-soaked, scourge-shredded back before his broken, beaten body was dashed on the cold dirt and the nails were pounded through his hands and feet with bone-pulverizing force.

Jesus did not live in a castle. Instead, he was born in a lowly stable, surrounded by the stink of damp hay and filthy (though adorable), strung-out animals. During his ministry, he had nowhere to call home and no place to rest his head. Christ, the king of heaven and earth, did not have servants attending to his every need. It was he who rather humbly got down on his hands and knees and washed the grime covered feet of his disciples. It was he who served others and taught us to do the same. The kingship of Jesus was and is a kingship of service, and this is the kingship we, too, are called to participate in. We, too, are called to help those in need and be attentive to how we can serve Christ in serving others. Don't forget, as our Lord said, "Whatsoever you do to the least of my brothers/sisters, that you do unto me." When we serve those in need, we serve Christ. When we ignore those in need, we ignore Christ.

THE COMMITMENT, RESPONSIBILITY, AND JOURNEY OF BAPTISM

TO GET BACK TO THE RITUAL now, following this anointing with Chrism, the individual is clothed with a white garment. The person being baptized, especially in the case of infants, will most likely have a white baptismal outfit of some kind already on. But still, the baby is given what, in many cases, looks like a white bib, whereas older children and adults are given a white robe to wear, or what looks like a white stole to put on. In any case, after the white garment is placed on the individual receiving the sacrament, the priest summarizes what has taken place thus far: "You have become a new creation in Christ, and have clothed yourself in Christ. See in this white garment the outward sign of your Christian dignity. With your family and friends to help you by word and example, bring that dignity unstained into the everlasting life of heaven."[9]

It's interesting to note that many of the same elements that are used at a baptism, such as water, fire (candle), and a white garment, are also used during a funeral. At a Catholic funeral, the casket of the faithful departed is draped in a white funeral pall. This signifies and brings to fulfillment the reality of what takes place at this moment during baptism when the child is given the white garment. The white pall reminds us that the deceased was baptized, that he was and is a child of God, that her earthly journey has ended, and that he hopefully will come before God "unstained into the everlasting life of heaven."[10] This is also why we need the sacrament of Reconciliation, to give us a good soul-washing when we get it "filthified" (that's a word I made up) with sin.

Next, someone from the family of the person being baptized lights a baptismal candle from the Easter candle as the priest explains, "Parents and godparents, this light is entrusted to you to be kept burning brightly. This child of yours has been enlightened by Christ. He/she is to walk always as a child of the light. May he/she keep the flame of faith alive in her/his heart. When the Lord comes, may he/she go out to meet him with all the saints in the heavenly kingdom."[11]

Here we see once more that a material element, fire, is being used to signify a sacred reality; in this case, it signifies the reality of the fire of the Holy Spirit, of God's light, truth, wisdom and the warmth of his love. We don't use all these things just because they look neat. Everything that is a part of Catholic liturgy is used for a reason: to express and enter into a sacred reality, and if that reality is not present, it should not be used. Liturgy is not a theatrical production put on for our entertainment; it draws us into the genuineness of the sacred and a true encounter with the Lord. Liturgy is our official worship of God Almighty and the means for the bestowal of his gift of grace. It's not meant to give us the cheap, fabricated emotional thrill of a Broadway musical.

So, as the ritual of baptism proceeds, after the candle is lit, the priest then touches the ears and mouth of the child and reminds those present of what Jesus did in the gospel when he made the deaf hear and the dumb speak. The priest asks the Lord to touch the ears of the child to receive God's word and the child's mouth to proclaim God's faith.

As the rite comes to a conclusion, the priest reminds those present of the sacramental path the child is destined to take, as he states, "Dearly beloved, this child has been reborn in Baptism. He/she is now called the child of God for so indeed he/she is. In Confirmation he/she will receive the fullness of God's spirit. In Holy Communion he/she will share the banquet of Christ's sacrifice, calling God his/her father in the midst of the Church. In the name of this child, in the Spirit of our common sonship, let us pray together in the words our Lord has given us."[12] And so, those present naturally do this by reciting the Our Father.

To wrap things up, a notable and quite beautiful blessing is given to the mother of the child, then the father of the child, and then one for all present. To put some icing on this tasty, sacramental cake, it is prescribed that a song of thanksgiving or a hymn to the Blessed Virgin Mary be sung to further express the joy of what has taken place. And with that, the Rite of Baptism comes to an end.

Ah yes . . . do you hear that? It's that trickling water once again. It's the cool, calming water that was poured over your head at the dawn of your spiritual life. It's still refreshing you, purifying you, nourishing you, and giving you courage and strength. Don't let it go dry! Every time you come to Mass and dip your hand in the Holy Water font, you remind yourself of what the water of your baptism has done and is continuing to do in your life as a child of God. It reminds you to take seriously, and live out to the fullest, your role as priest, prophet, and king. That water has transformed you into a child of God and made you a member of his family. So, be a good son or daughter, love your family, and let the grace that came with that water continue to transform you into the "new creature" that God desires you to be!

CHAPTER 4

THE SPIRITUAL GARBAGE MAN

GOD BLESS THE GARBAGE MAN! It's a hard, dirty job, but as they say, somebody has to do it. Life would be quite different for us without the service of those brave men and women who, day in and day out, haul away our refuse. Just imagine if they weren't around. Think of all the piled-up filth that would surround your home or apartment. We'd be living in squalor, with decaying food and putrid juices oozing out all around us. The stink in our neighborhoods would be on par with the bowels of hell! Just think about all the diseased, dirty rats running around, sneaking about while feasting their trash-eating faces on all that delicious discard! Oh, how their beady little eyes would teem with delight at the notion of living among us and making themselves the kings of our waste wonderland.

Now imagine also that in addition to our food waste and the immediate corruptible garbage we get rid of every day, there was no means of throwing away all the other junk we go through. We'd truly become the victims (as we already are, really) of our throw-away society. There'd be old TVs and computer monitors, stacked up like brick walls along the streets, and boxes of broken-down plastic gadgets strewn about. Old sofas and junk furniture that isn't made to last through the weekend would be piled up in massive mounds like great obelisks reaching to the sky in praise to our gods of materialism and consumerism.

To finish off this imaginary refuse resort, think if we couldn't get rid of all the empty bottles, cans, bags, jugs, newspapers, magazines and yard waste that we go through on a weekly basis. With no way to get rid of our garbage, it would truly be hell on earth! We'd literally be living in Gehenna (the burning trash pit Jesus refers to in describing hell). We'd be forced to eat the rotten fruit of our own lavishness and wastefulness. Our consumption and greed would materialize right before our eyes, and it would in return consume us! We'd find ourselves trapped, wallowing in the belly of the beast of excessiveness, slowly being digested by our own rubbish. Not to mention, in the mean time, we'd all be riddled with sickness and disease, and the plague would probably break out again. Cheery thought, isn't it?

So again I say, God bless the garbage man! Lord knows how we take him for granted. No doubt about it, without our refuse system in place to remove and process our trash, life would be very, very different. You know what, though? This horrific fantasy is a reality for many people spiritually. For too many people, the waste produced by their consumption of evil — sin, that is — has piled up to the point that it has negatively affected and altered the nature of their lives and of their very being. It has poisoned them. It has piled up and surrounded their souls, blocking out the grace of God. It has made their lives a miserable mockery of what it could and should be, and the true horror is that many don't even realize it.

SPIRITUAL TRASH AND THE SACRAMENT
OF RECONCILIATION

LIKE PIGS WHO ARE perfectly happy in you-know-what, we too can become conditioned to accept the filth in our lives as the norm. With our faces in the dirt and our eyes focused down in

the muck, we fail to look up and see all the beauty
that God has in store for us and wants us to expe
only come to him and be washed clean, if we coul
of all that spiritual garbage that has held us captive ~~~ ~~~~ ~~~
souls.

Well, the good news is that one can get rid of all that sin.
There is a way to have it hauled off and taken away forever. God
is standing by with the soap and water to scrub clean even the
grimiest of his children. It's a little something we call the sacrament of Reconciliation. Going to confession is how we take out
the trash of our spiritual lives, and the priest who administers the
sacrament is your very own spiritual garbage man.

There has always been a lot of misunderstanding about the
sacrament of Reconciliation on the part of non-Catholics and
Catholics alike. "Why do I need to go to a priest? Why can't I just
confess my sins directly to God? What's the deal with doing a
penance?" These are just a few of the common questions that arise
concerning Reconciliation that we'll look at. So without further
ado, let me teach you how to properly take out the trash.

For starters, as we've already learned, a sacrament is not just
a symbolic re-enactment of something, but a *real* experience of
God's grace established by Jesus for that very purpose. In Scripture we see that Jesus called people to repentance, and he forgave
the sins of those who showed true sorrow. We also see that Jesus
gave his *chosen* disciples (priests) the very real mission and power
to "bind and loose" sins. He gave them the authority to forgive in
his name. However, in the gospel there is no specific ritual laid out
for reconciliation. This is something that has developed and
evolved with time as a part of our Sacred Tradition.

For the early Christians, there was great importance placed
on confessing one's sins to the entire community and not wor-
shiping with a guilty conscience. Sin does, after all, affect

everybody, not just the sinner. We all suffer the consequences of each others' sin. It has a tremendous domino effect and can start a chain reaction of sin. Being aware of this, those first Catholics knew it was good not just to confess sins individually, but to say "I'm sorry" to everyone. And so, things like fasting, giving to the poor, fraternal correction, and praying for each other began to be seen as a way to imitate Christ, to develop a more virtuous life, and to "make up," or repair, the damage caused by one's sins. This is basically what penance is.

A few centuries later, a more formalized method of public reconciliation came about. Those who were excommunicated (kicked out of the Church because of grave and very serious sin) could now go to the bishop (after they reformed their lives) and ask for forgiveness and re-admittance into the Church. As a sign of their being readmitted, the bishop would impose his hands on them, which was the beginning of the ritualized sacrament that eventually came about.

There were a few problems that arose from this more ritualized procedure. In some cases, things got out of hand. Some were being assigned public penances that were very long and overly demanding. Let me remind you that scandalous clerical abuse has come in many forms throughout the centuries. It is certainly nothing new.

With more and more problems arising in the development of the sacrament, St. Augustine and his contemporaries took to heart and applied the understanding as found in Matthew's gospel that a priest, as successor to the apostles, has the authority to forgive sins. With the emphasis being placed more on the scriptural roots of the sacrament, the practice of individual confessions began emerging. This practice grew rapidly as a result of Irish missionary monks who implemented this method among the people they served. In order to achieve an element of fairness in their ministry, the monks began to develop a system of certain penances for certain sins. This practice grew and spread throughout Europe, and in 650 at the council of Chalon, individual confession to a priest was approved.

But, of course, things couldn't be left alone. Once again, theological debates ensued in an attempt to explain things such as: What *precisely* is the nature of the sacrament of Penance? In order to clarify things, the great saint and theologian St. Thomas Aquinas established a notion of the matter and form (the what and the how) of the sacrament of Penance. He concluded that the matter of the sacrament was made up of the actions of the priest as well as the penitent: the penitent expressed sorrow for his or her sins and confessed them; the priest listened to the confession, issued a penance, and gave absolution. The form of the sacrament, then, was found in the words of absolution.

It is important to point out that individual confession, while being a private encounter between God, priest, and person (penitent), does have a communal nature. The priest, who acts in the person of Jesus, also represents the community. Quite often, the priest will give a penance that involves praying or doing something for the community. And so, when one confesses his or her sins, it is not just confessing to Jesus (through the priest), but in fact admitting sins to the entire Body of Christ (the Church). This reality also takes place at Mass during the penitential rite when we, out loud, admit that we are sinners and ask God to "have mercy on us."

Many Catholics think that when they commit a sin, all they need to do is just walk outside, look up to the sky, say, "Sorry, God," and be on their merry way. Though it is important to recognize our sins and to say we are sorry, Jesus desires for us to have an *experience* of forgiveness. He wants us to put our money where our mouth is. He wants us to actually come before him, to speak out loud the wrong we have done, to make amends, to be healed, to truly be forgiven, and *then* go on our merry way. To be able to speak aloud the sins we have committed means to take real ownership of them and no longer make excuses for ourselves. To have the humility and courage to bring our faults and failings before the Lord and the community (represented by the priest), in a very *real* way, takes guts and conviction! To hear the words, "I forgive you," spoken back to you by a person that Jesus himself gave the authority to forgive sin, is an incredible, powerful, healing, freeing experience of the mercy and love of God. This is why we have the sacrament of Reconciliation. This is why God has given it to us. To not take advantage of it, is, well, to be blunt, just plain lazy and stupid. And, as with all the sacraments, Reconciliation bestows the grace of God upon us that really does give us the courage and strength to live a more Christ-like life and avoid sin. To miss out on all this good stuff is utterly foolish.

THE NATURE AND EFFECTS OF SIN AND EVIL

LET'S TALK FOR A BIT now about sin itself. Pope John Paul II once said that the loss of the sense of sin goes hand in hand with the loss of the sense of God. This is an obvious phenomenon in our culture. There are other reasons, though, as to why so many have little or no sense of the sin and evil in their lives. One of the biggest reasons is that we are bombarded constantly with immorality. We have been desensitized by it. We have allowed ourselves to be conditioned to accept it as the norm.

Every evening on prime-time TV, one can see adultery, promiscuity, theft, violence, and everything in between. The Lord's name being used in vain flows freely through the airwaves and into our homes. Magazine covers at the grocery checkout lane stare us in the face with half-naked women and articles about how to not get caught cheating on your boyfriend, have better sex, make use of the latest birth control devices, and how to dress like a tramp. Of course, all the same stuff is glorified in popular music, movies, morning radio programs, and so on. Literally everywhere we look, we will be assaulted by immorality. Many young (and not-so-young) people spend hours upon hours playing very realistic video games where the goal is to mercilessly gun down as many individuals as one can in the most bloody, graphic manner possible. Is it any wonder that troubled, mentally ill youth then go to school and do it for real? They've been practicing every day for years at home or in the dorm room.

The result, of course, is that this barrage of immorality slowly chisels away at our fortitude and moral integrity, slowly weakening our values. There is an old adage about boiling a frog that accurately describes our current situation. If you put a frog in a pot of boiling water, he'll jump right out, but if you put him in some lukewarm water and very slowly bring it to a boil, he'll stay right there and get cooked to death! The same thing is happening to us. We remain complacent and apathetic as the evil in our culture and in our lives reaches a boiling point and stews us alive like a succulent Maine lobster to be feasted upon by the devil himself!

For those who try to remain vigilant in the fight against the soul-destroying venom of our society, there is also the danger of compartmentalizing our spirituality. We can live our lives as if it were contained in a divider box. In one little box we have our relationship with God, in the other is our family life, the other our work, and the other our play. It can be easy to keep them separate and disjointed, thus failing to include God in everything we do. We can find ourselves going to church on Sunday, then putting God on the back burner (out of our lives) while we contradict all that we say we believe with our actions and words the rest of the week.

God wants to be included in every aspect of our lives so that we may give glory to him in all that we do, so that we may seek his guidance in all areas, that we may be a witness and example for others at all times and in all things. The more we place God as the focus and center of our lives, the stronger and better we become as human beings and as God's children. The more we realize God's presence, the more we also come to realize how sinful we truly are and how much we need God's forgiveness and healing.

So what exactly is sin, you may ask. The textbook definition of sin is: "It is an offense against reason, truth, and right conscience; it is a failure in genuine love for God and neighbor caused by attachment to certain goods" (CCC 1849). Sin is rooted in disobedience to God, which is how it entered into the world. Sin weakens, and in some cases destroys, our relationship with God and with others. It separates us from God's love and grace. It is a failure to keep God's commands. God does not *command* us to avoid certain things because he wants to take the fun and excitement out of our lives, but rather because he loves us, and he knows that if we do certain things, we will make our lives and our world a miserable place. Check out the morning paper and see for yourself.

Let's take a closer look at that issue of disobedience for a second. You know, many in our culture think that the ability to exercise disobedience is an act of freedom. We hear people say, "I have the *freedom* to have an abortion. I have the *liberty* to do whatever I want sexually. I can worship God as *I* see fit." Many talk of being *free* from traditional family values and being *liberated* from the teachings of the Church. It's interesting to note, as many a Scripture scholar has pointed out, that throughout the Bible, whenever the word "liberation" or "freedom" is used, it is a reference to things that are evil. Scripture talks about *freedom* from sin and of being *liberated* from the captivity of death. Being freed and liberated from things that are good isn't a good thing!

Society has completely reversed and manipulated the true meaning of freedom and liberation. True freedom is the ability to choose what is good and reject what is evil. It is the ability to say "no" to things that enslave us. The philosopher G.W.F. Hegel came up with what is known as the *Master-Slave dialectic*, and though this model can be used to make all sorts of points, I often refer to it in regard to sin. In the relationship of a master and a slave, the master is dependent upon the slave to do the work he needs done, while the slave is dependent upon the master for food, shelter, clothing, and, essentially, life. Over time, though, if the master becomes too dependent upon the slave, he loses his freedom and, in essence, becomes the slave while the slave has, in fact, become the master.

To give a clearer example of this master-slave phenomenon, take a look at someone who is addicted to cigarettes (not to pick on you smokers): Johnny decides to take up smoking. He chose to buy a pack of smokes and, well, start smoking. Johnny is the "master." He decided how, when, and why to use cigarettes. He is in control. The cigarettes, meanwhile, are the "slave." They are simply there to be used for the master's pleasure and have no power whatsoever. Over time, though, Johnny becomes addicted to cigarettes. He can no longer do without them, and he no longer has the *freedom* to choose how, when, or why to smoke. Now, he *has* to smoke, and it is killing him. Now, Johnny is the slave to his cigarettes, who have become the master.

A similar thing happens by means of our sinfulness. I heard it said once that sin is like an addictive substance for the soul. The more of it that is in us, the harder it is for us to break free of it. And so, the more we choose to do the wrong thing, the more we choose to disobey God and sin, the harder it is to break away from that sin. We find ourselves truly enslaved and addicted (to varying degrees) to things like lying, cheating, stealing, sexual immorality, lustful thinking, losing our temper, using God's name in vain, etc. We lose our freedom to say "no" to those things, and meanwhile, they make our lives and the lives of others miserable. They don't free us or liberate us; they chain and shackle us. We become prisoners of our own sinfulness.

Obedience to God truly keeps us free, on the right track, and able to enjoy life to the fullest. God knows this; that's why he asks us to be obedient to him. Think of it in terms of being on a basketball team. If your team is in the final minutes of the big championship game and your coach, who knows what he's doing, tells you to break right during the final play, and you say, "To heck with that . . . I'm going to go left," what do you think is going to happen? Your team will most likely not make good on the game-winning play and you'll go home a big, fat loser! And all because you were disobedient to your coach. The same applies to our spiritual life. God is our coach, he knows what he's doing, and he asks that we listen to him if we are going to win the game of life and celebrate that victory in heaven.

Sin is an act of disobedience that nullifies our true freedom, and it also brings about evil. One of the ways that evil can be defined is this: it is the choosing of something that is initially good, in a way that is not so good, in a disordered way. Transportation, for example, is a good thing. It's good to be able to get around and take care of the things we need to do: to get to work, to run errands, visit folks, to go on trips, etc. Having a vehicle for transportation is a good thing. Now if my truck broke down, I would need a new one to get around and do my job. For me to go out in the church parking lot on Sunday morning and take (steal) whichever vehicle I wanted would obviously not be good. I would have broken the law, I would have made the owner very angry, I would go to jail, and, of course, I would have broken one of God's commandments. All this because I wanted something good (transportation) but willfully chose to get it in a disordered (bad) way.

A more poignant example of moral evil would be sexual activity outside of marriage. Sexual intercourse is a good thing; it is a gift from God. It is (supposed to be) the ultimate expression of love. It is an act that unifies a man and women physically and spiritually and has the possibility (and is naturally ordered towards) of bringing new life into the world. To choose to be sexually active in a situation where there is no commitment, or even love for that matter, where there is the possibility of disease, death, unwanted pregnancy, or a multitude of other dreaded consequences, is obviously not a good thing — it is evil, it is a sin.

As the reader may or may not know, there are two kinds of sin, there is mortal sin and venial sin. Venial sin is that which weakens but does not break our relationship with God or others. They are "small mistakes" one could say, but nonetheless are still not right and good. They still do have a negative effect on us, God, and others. Venial sins are things like telling a "white lie," stealing a few bucks, disobeying one's parents, treating people with disrespect, being jealous and envious of others, eating too much, being lazy, cheating, etc. They are things that we know we shouldn't do, but still do anyhow, or may even do without realizing we've done it.

Mortal sin, on the other hand, is that which breaks our relationship with God and others. It throws away the grace of God that is present in our lives and can only be forgiven by means of sacramental confession. Committing a mortal sin is like purposely ripping out our Christian dignity and flushing it down the toilet. It extinguishes the fire of God's love and presence in our souls. For a mortal sin to be a mortal sin, three things have to take place: it has to be a grave and serious matter, we have to know it is a serious matter, and we have to do it freely. Mortal sins are things such as adultery, murder, promiscuity, abortion, artificial contraception, masturbation, getting blind drunk or abusing drugs (which destroys the will), using pornography (participating in the dehumanization of others), missing Mass on Sunday (rejecting the gift of our salvation that Jesus died for), and things of that nature. It's important to point out that in the case of addiction, the gravity of things that would be considered a mortal sin is lessened because the person no longer has willful control — he or she has become a slave to an evil master and has given up his or her freedom. However, that individual is responsible to seek help to overcome this addiction.

Sin breaks us down, weakens us, and holds us hostage. It keeps us from being the people that God wants us to be. But through the forgiveness God offers us in the sacrament of Reconciliation, we can be healed and restored. When we are willing to seek forgiveness, and to forgive others, we break the chains of evil that hold us captive. But for us to truly take advantage of all this, to truly throw out our spiritual garbage, we have to be aware of and recognize what that garbage is; we have to properly use our conscience.

THE CONSCIENCE

OUR CONSCIENCE IS A GREAT GIFT that God has given us. It is an imperative tool that we use to avoid sin and do the right thing. However, if our conscience is not properly formed, it is useless. It simply becomes a matter of making decisions based on our feelings, which often deceive us, rather than on the objective truth of right and wrong as God has revealed it to us. Having an ill-formed conscience is like being color blind. As our eyes have deteriorated, or lost their ability to perceive true color, a light may begin to look green, while in reality it's actually red, and when we run that red light due to misperception, we get smashed by the oncoming traffic.

Sin also plays a big part in the use of our conscience. The more sin we have in our life and the longer we go without recognizing it, repenting of it, and confessing it, the more our conscience is disintegrated and rendered powerless. Thus the vital importance of a properly formed conscience, which is a three-step process of informing, reforming, and conforming.

We inform our conscience by means of being taught right from wrong. This usually (hopefully) takes place, for the most part, when we are children. Our parents, teachers, preachers, etc., help us to learn good from evil and to strive for the good. It is also, in most cases, a rather natural process. That "little voice in the back of our heads" keeps us on the right path, if we've learned to listen to it. It's not just a one-time thing, though. We are to continue to inform our consciences all our lives, by staying up to date on the ethical and moral issues of our current time, by paying attention and seeking to truly understand the teachings of Christ and his Church. We should never stop seeking the truth and striving for goodness as we go through life. It's important to do our homework, or at least get our information from trustworthy sources, *not* from your local Church-hating newspaper or jaded, biased news program! Get your information about the Church from the Church (or at least those approved by her)!

To reform our conscience means to take personal responsibility for our decisions, which is a rare thing these days. Everybody is a victim; everybody has an excuse; it's always somebody else's fault. We see this in the thousands of frivolous lawsuits that we hear about: A lady burns herself with coffee that *she* spilled, so she sues the restaurant. A burglar breaks through a window, cuts himself on the glass, and sues the homeowner. A driver sues an automobile manufacturer after he crashed his car and was injured, because he was too drunk to figure out how to put the seat belt on. Nobody puts a gun to our head and *makes* us sin; if that were the case, it wouldn't be a sin. Though temptation certainly gets the best of us at times, we make the decision, it's our responsibility, and it's our job to face the atonal music that we've composed for ourselves by our poor decisions and selfishness.

Finally, we must conform our conscience. This is basically the process of constantly striving to do the will of God in our lives. And the basic will of God is the same for all of us: it is to love God, love others, and avoid sin, which destroys that love.

One of the greatest ways to keep ourselves in check is to examine our consciences on a regular basis — that is, to assess our actions in accordance with our faith and with God's will. It is a process of holding ourselves accountable, keeping tabs on our decisions and actions, and recognizing whether we have truly strived for good or whether we have let ourselves fall into sin.

An examination of conscience can and should be done daily. It really doesn't take much time. It's simply a matter of taking a few moments, looking over our day, recognizing the good, identifying the not-so-good, and committing to willfully make improvements in those not-so-good areas. A more extensive, thorough examination should be done before one comes to Confession, but whether one is going to Confession or just doing a daily checkup, a simple and effective way to do an examination of conscience is to go through the Ten Commandments.

THE TEN COMMANDMENTS AND
EXAMINATION OF CONSCIENCE

Just a quick word about the Ten Commandments while we're on the subject. There are some Christian denominations out there who teach that Jesus abolished the Ten Commandments. This is absolutely false! Jesus spoke very clearly on several occasions about keeping them. In Matthew 5:17-19, we hear Jesus say,

"Think not that I have come to abolish the law and the prophets; I have come not to abolish them but to fulfil them. For truly, I say to you, till heaven and earth pass away, not an iota, not a dot, will pass from the law until all is accomplished. Whoever, then relaxes one of the least of these commandments and teaches men so, shall be called least in the kingdom of heaven; but he who does them and teaches them shall be called great in the kingdom of heaven."

Later, in Matthew 19:16-17, we hear the story of the rich young man asking Jesus, "Teacher, what good deed must I do, to have eternal life?" And, in response, Jesus says, "If you would enter life, keep the commandments." Our Lord goes on to recall a few of them that concern love of neighbor: "You shall not kill, You shall not commit adultery, You shall not steal, You shall not bear false witness, Honor your father and mother..." Eventually, in Matthew 22:37-39, Jesus sums up these commandments with the Great Commandment, "You shall love the Lord your God with all your heart, and with all your soul, and with all your mind," and a second like it, "You shall love your neighbor as yourself."

Jesus also challenges the rich young man in Matthew 19 to "Go, sell what you possess and give to the poor, and you will have treasure in heaven; and come, follow me" (Mt 19:21). This instruction, along with the Great Commandment, does not do away with keeping the law of the Commandments. It is rather an invitation to discover the person (Jesus) who is the perfect fulfillment and embodiment of them. Jesus' message was to live the law of the Ten Commandments out of love, which is the spirit in which they were given. It is only we who have perceived them in a negative fashion, as a list of demanding "don't do's."

Those who claim that Jesus abolished the Ten Commandments often point to passages from St. Paul where he speaks of followers of Christ being free from the law. The "law" that he is speaking of here is the Mosaic Law, the enormous list of rules, regulations, judgments, social precepts, etc. that are found in the Torah. And yes, as St. Paul points out and fundamentalists proclaim, Christians are not bound to live under the Jewish (Mosaic) law. But the *Decalogue* (Ten Commandments), which are found in the Torah, were written by the very "Finger of God." (Ex 31:18; Deut 5:22), and thus apply to all God's people for all time, of which again, Jesus was the perfect embodiment. I could go on and on here with explaining things further, but hopefully you get the point. For further study, read paragraphs 2052-2074 of the *Catechism of the Catholic Church*.

To get back on track now, the following is a sample of questions that one could reflect on for each commandment as a means of examining one's conscience. I've been adding onto, using, and referring people to this particular examination for years, but I'm not sure who actually put it together or where it came from, so whoever you are, great job!

COMMANDMENT #1
I am the Lord your God; you shall not have strange gods before me.

- Do we truly love God above all, or do we sometimes give greater importance to things of this world: money, image, looks, clothes, popularity, or selfish desires?
- Do we claim to have good values, but often bend or abandon them under pressure?
- Do we turn to God in thankful prayer, or do we pray mostly when we want something?
- Do we really want to be transformed by the will of God, or do we just use our religion in order to look good?

COMMANDMENT #2
You shall not take the name of the Lord in vain.

- Do we show disrespect for God's name by misusing it out of frustration or anger, or to get attention from others?
- Do we hesitate to mention God's name in appropriate situations, in conversations with friends and family members?
- Do we strive to continue to learn about God by paying attention in Church, religion class, or through other educational opportunities?

COMMANDMENT #3
Remember to keep holy the Lord's Day.

- Do we come to Church to celebrate the Eucharist on Sundays and Holy Days?
- Do we attend Mass only when it is convenient or when it will make us feel good?
- Do we participate in the Eucharist by praying and singing, or do we simply sit as spectators and wait to be entertained?
- Do we pay close attention to the Word of God and open ourselves to God's call to allow his word to take effect in our lives?
- Do we acknowledge the "true presence" of Christ in the Eucharist and receive Holy Communion with respect and reverence?

COMMANDMENT #4
Honor your father and your mother.

- Do we help bring peace and happiness to our families, or are we disrespectful of others and become a source of hurt and division for those who are closest to us?

- As parents, are we generous and patient with our children? Do we spend time with them and give them the attention they need? Do we set responsible limits for them and make sure they follow rules that will help them grow into responsible adults?

- Are we willing to say "no" to our children, or are we more likely to ignore problem behavior and hope it will "go away?"

- Do we listen to our children carefully and treat them with respect?

- As children, do we love, and are we respectful and obedient to our parents? Do we appreciate the many sacrifices they make for us? Do we say "Thank you" and "I love you" often enough?

- Do we do our chores without being asked, or do we wait for our parents to become upset before we move away from what we are doing?

- Do we listen to our parents' reasoning when they say "no" to us?

COMMANDMENT #5
You shall not kill.

- Have we injured another person through carelessness or fighting?

- Have we placed others or ourselves in danger because of reckless use of alcohol or other drugs? Have we caused difficulties for ourselves or others because of their use?

- Have we risked our lives by driving or riding with someone under the influence of alcohol or other drugs?

- Do we strive to forgive those who have hurt us, or do we hold on to resentment and desire for revenge?

- Do we use our powers of influence well, especially our voting rights, in order to fight war, oppression, abortion, and injustice, or do we allow those evils to continue by our apathy and our silence? Have we been violent or abusive either in action or in speech?

- Have we been verbally abusive to our children or other family members?

- Do we share what we have with those in need? Do we support the life and mission of the Church by responsible stewardship, by sharing our time, talent and treasure?

- Do we bring our Christianity to every day situations, or do we stand on the sidelines and complain about every flaw we can detect in others?

COMMANDMENT #6
You shall not commit adultery.

- Do we respect the dignity of the human body and the holiness of Christian marriage? Do we show that respect in our speech, or are crude language and jokes often part of our conversations?

- Do we understand and appreciate the gift of our sexuality as a means of expressing our love (and God's love) in the sacrament of Marriage?

- Have we been faithful to our marriage, priestly, or religious vows? Do we keep our commitments simply because we said we would, or do we seek to nourish ourselves and others through our lifetime commitments?
- Have we dishonored our bodies by fornication, impurity, or unworthy conversation or thought leading to impure actions?
- Have we encouraged others to sin by our failure to maintain good moral standards?

COMMANDMENT #7
You shall not steal.

- Do we respect the property of other people? Have we stolen, damaged, or vandalized the property of others?
- Have we cheated at work or in school? Have we encouraged others to sin by pressuring them into helping us cheat?
- Are we honest and hardworking in school and at work?
- Are we faithful to our promises? Can we be trusted?

COMMANDMENT #8
You shall not bear false witness against your neighbor.

- Have we lied to stay out of trouble or to avoid a difficult situation?
- Do we gossip about others? Have we damaged the reputation of another person by exaggeration or making up stories about them?
- Can we be trusted with a secret?
- Do we stand up for those unjustly accused, or are we merely a channel through which rumors pass, whether or not they are true?

COMMANDMENT #9
You shall not covet your neighbor's wife.

- Have we weakened or damaged our marriage commitment through our obsession with another person?
- Do we respect the commitments of others and help them remain faithful to their promises?
- Do we treat our marriages casually in our conversations and attitudes? Have we said or done anything that made a mockery of our sacred promises?

COMMANDMENT #10
You shall not covet your neighbor's goods.

- Are we satisfied with what God has given us, or are we jealous of those who seem to have more?
- Do we try to prove we are better than others by bragging or buying more things?
- Do we appreciate our own good qualities, or do we constantly compare ourselves with others and become resentful or bitter?
- Do we cope well with the problems that confront us and maintain our Christian hope in spite of hard times and difficulties?
- Do we truly "seek first the Kingdom of God" in our lives and place our trust in Him?
- Do we reflect the peace, hope and joy of a people redeemed and made holy by the Blood of Christ?

This is a fairly extensive examination, as you can see, and it would be a great one to go through before going to the sacrament of Reconciliation, but again, for daily use, one can simplify things quite a bit.

So what happens next after we've identified our sins? The next step is to repent. To repent means to humbly come before God, to honestly recognize our weaknesses and sinfulness, to actively turn away from them and turn our lives over more fully to the Lord. After having done this, you're ready to load up those trash cans and take out the garbage in the sacrament of Reconciliation.

GOING TO CONFESSION

WHEN ONE COMES to the sacrament, it is naturally assumed that the penitent (that's you) has done a thorough examination of conscience, is truly sorry for his or her sins, has repented of them, and truly intends to avoid those things in the future. I'm always kind of mystified when someone comes to the sacrament of Reconciliation after a twenty-year layoff and tells me, "Well, I guess I told a few lies . . . and . . . uh . . . I guess that's it." So again, do a *thorough* examination of conscience.

After getting properly prepared, a basic confession goes like this: Come in and greet (and be greeted) by the priest. The most common greeting is, "Forgive me, Father, for I have sinned." By the way, it's up to you whether you want to go face to face or go behind the screen. Next, tell him approximately when your last confession was, what your state of life is (married, single, etc.), and then confess your sins. Don't try to hide anything and make a play on words to avoid the truth of what you've done, you're only hurting yourself by not being honest, and we know anyway. We're familiar with every sin-disguising trick and technique there is, so tell the truth and get rid of *all* that garbage!

After confessing your sins, the priest may give you some counsel to help you with what you have been struggling with, or he may not. Not all priests are gifted confessors — some are very straightforward and to the point, and others are more detailed and conversational in their administration of the sacrament. Keep in mind, too, that Confession is not necessarily a counseling session. If you want to discuss things in more detail (or if the priest recommends it), that should be done at another time when there are not other people patiently waiting to also receive the sacrament. After confessing your sins and receiving some possible advice, the priest will give a penance. Every priest gives different kinds of penances. Some give the penance of saying a certain amount of certain prayers for a certain intention; others will give a penance that is related to the sin itself as a way of making future improvements. Others may assign acts of charity or service or things along those lines.

After the penance is assigned, the penitent should recite the Act of Contrition, a prayer in which one expresses sorrow for his or her sins and asks for God's grace and help in the future. There are many versions out there, or one can make up his or her own. After that, the priest says the prayer of absolution and finishes with a "Go in peace" farewell. After Confession, the penitent should spend some time in prayer and perform the assigned penance (if it can be done immediately).

People always have lots of questions about things concerning making a good confession, so let me address a few while I'm at it. First of all, nothing one confesses (and I mean *absolutely nothing*) will shock or embarrass the priest. We've heard it all! So don't worry about that. Also, keep in mind that a priest can never, ever, under penalty of excommunication, publicly reveal anything that one confesses; he can never break that sacred "seal of Confession." What is said in the confessional stays in the confessional and will never see the light of day, period!

In regard to this seal of Confession, some ask, "What if someone confesses something like murder? Do you mean to tell me that the priest can't call the police and bring this person to justice? Isn't that a horrible sin as well?" In this case it is true that the priest still cannot reveal this person's sin or identity. The seal of Confession is absolute and cannot be broken no matter how horrible the sin. *But*, and *very importantly*, in such a case, I (and most priests I would think) would give that person the penance of turning him- or herself in. If the person is truly sorry for the sin and has a real desire for forgiveness and reconciliation, then he or she simply must take responsibility for the action. His or her absolution would depend upon it.

Another issue that comes up is concern about past sins or forgotten sins. If one comes to the sacrament with a truly contrite heart, with genuine sorrow for *all* of one's sins, then all of those sins are forgiven. When one walks out that confessional door, that person has a clean slate. As I pointed out earlier, one should never intentionally hide or disguise something, and every effort should be made to recall and confess every sin that one is aware of, but there are things we do forget. A good practice is to simply mention that you are sorry for *all* of your sins, even the ones you forget, after you've mentioned all the sins you can remember.

Another thing folks wrestle with is committing the same sins over and over again. People sometimes say to me, "Father, what's the use!? I just keep committing the same sins again and again!" My response is always to then come to Confession again and again. All of us have particular crosses we carry and sins that do come back repetitively. Many people struggle with the same sins for most of their lives. We are all prone to struggle in particular areas; for some, it's honesty; for others, it's lack of charity; and for someone else, it might be an addiction of some kind. The important thing is to get right back up after we're knocked into the ditch of sin and get right back on track. The longer we stay down, the harder it is to get back up. St. Augustine once said that our sins can be stepping-stones to God's grace. By means of our failures, we realize all the more how much we need the Lord's help and grace.

And grace is what it is all about. You'll get sick of hearing this from me, but grace is very real! It is the lifeblood of our spiritual being! It gives us the strength and motivation to avoid sin and do good. The more of it one has, the more one realizes how true this is. One will become aware of situations in which he or she suddenly has extra courage and strength to avoid temptation where in the past they would easily crumble like an old, stale, oatmeal cookie that's been laying around out on the parking lot for weeks on end.

This free giving out of God's grace is the reason to make frequent use of the sacrament of Reconciliation. I like to use the analogy of going to the dentist. If one avoids a dentist checkup for a long period of time (like I admittedly used to), when he finally goes, he may very well discover a multitude of problems that he never knew existed (like I did). With regular checkups, those problems stay under control, and one's teeth remain in good health (hopefully!). Spiritually speaking, if we go for long periods of time without Confession, we can become plagued with many sinful habits and tendencies that have crept into our lives and have been doing a fair (or great) amount of damage. Regular Confession is a great way to keep ourselves spiritually healthy and fortified with that ever-important grace.

So how often should one go to Confession? As Catholics, we are required to go annually. Canon 989 states, "All the faithful who have reached the age of discretion are bound faithfully to confess their graver sins at least once a year." Some go every six months, some go every few weeks, some go more, some go less. I recommend once a month as a good starting point. Personally, I feel that once a year just doesn't cut it. We certainly wouldn't take out the garbage only once a year. And that is what it's all about, getting rid of the trash in your soul, in your heart, and on your mind. The sacrament of Reconciliation is there for you and me as a constant invitation to experience God's mercy, grace, and purifying love. So don't be shy, round up all that filth, go pay a visit to a spiritual garbage man near you, and take out that trash! I guarantee that you'll be glad you did!

CHAPTER 5

THIS *IS* MY BODY.
THIS *IS* MY BLOOD.

ONE PARTICULAR SUMMER, in my younger days, I found myself working in a greasy fast-food restaurant. It was actually a big step down from my job at another eating establishment where I worked for three years while in high school. At the fast-food joint, I wasn't able to eat lunch for free, and I had to wear a demeaning, ridiculous outfit that made me feel like a court jester complete with a foolish paper hat and a big girly apron. The names of our products were so imbecilic that I genuinely felt a little vindicated when the hungry customers had to actually speak the words out loud. They'd always seem to look over their shoulders before they muttered in a low voice with shifty eyes, "Uhhh . . . I'd like a Jumbo Johnny Queen Burger, an order of Slick Dandy Fries, and a Mega Choco-bitty Surprise Shake." I could never hold back the slight, satisfied smirk that would slowly ease across my face upon hearing the names of such culinary tomfoolery.

I recall that on one particular Friday evening, things were very slow and the few of us who were working that night were just kind of off in our own worlds as we went about polishing the stainless steel counters and tidying things up. Finally, after what seemed like an eternity, a customer came along and ordered some food. That night I was working back in the kitchen, and so I went about the task of making the burger, wrapping it up, and sending it down the little chute to my coworkers on the other side of the great grease divide.

After all that excitement I went back to the mundane task of sweeping the floor for the hundredth time. A few minutes later the same customer came back in with a surprised and troubled look on her face. She slowly made her way up to the counter and asked to speak to the manager. Out of the little room in the back where the managers would dwell, a cloud of cigarette smoke and the angst-ridden sounds of Led Zeppelin emerged out of the quickly opened and closed door as my manager made his way to the front counter. A the manager's kind greeting, the customer carefully took her sandwich out of the soggy paper bag and unwrapped it as if she were displaying the remains of a deceased pet. She then began to recount the episode that had just taken place. "Well, sir, I just came in here a few minutes ago to order a Jimmy-Fist Deluxe Burger, and after I started eating, I realized that the actual burger part was missing." She then meticulously pried open the burger bun that was sealed shut with mayonnaise, ketchup, and other sundry goos, to reveal that indeed, there was no meat present.

Somehow in the malaise of the evening's doldrums I simply forgot to put the meat on the bun. And for a burger that was supposed to have two huge meat patties the size of a monkey's fist, it just didn't go over too well with the customer. I didn't blame her, of course. So with great embarrassment and that slight smirk on my face, I quickly remedied the situation and dispatched a new burger, complete with meat this time.

That episode became the source of a good many jokes that were pointed in my direction. I just might have unknowingly invented the first vegetarian burger! But really, what is a hamburger without the meat? Well, I'll tell you, it's nothing, that's what it is. Everything else on the burger is designed to deliver the meat to one's gullet with enthused celebration and mechanical efficiency! The cheese helps provide a protective surface that keeps the pickle juice from entering the pores of the meat patty. The bun soaks up the extra grease so that it doesn't coat one's esophagus on the way down the hatch. The ketchup, mayonnaise, and mustard hold the whole thing together so that it doesn't erupt too quickly into a big fistful of slop while driving down the highway. The onions give it a bitter bite so as to remind one of the price the cow paid, and the wrapping paper is essentially the shroud of death that pays homage to your lunch/dinner break.

Meat is the protein-packed heart and soul of a hamburger. A hamburger without meat is like a guitar without strings, like a plane without wings, and like dents without the dings. The meat of the hamburger is the source and the summit of the fast-food empire! That compressed puck of ground beef is the cornerstone for which all else is laid upon and revolves around. Without it, we cry out in a loud, demanding voice (like the old lady in the popular commercial back in the '80s) . . . "Where's the beef!?"

THE EUCHARIST AS THE SOURCE AND SUMMIT OF OUR FAITH

FOR US AS CATHOLICS, the Church teaches that the Eucharist is the "source and summit" of our faith and of our lives as Christians. All the other sacraments and all the other work and ministry that the Church is involved with are rooted in the Eucharist. The Eucharist is the "meat" of our faith. I often hear non-Catholics say things like, "What's the deal with all this Eucharist stuff? You all talk about 'celebrating' the Eucharist, 'receiving' the Eucharist, 'adoring' the Eucharist, and so on. What gives?"

It is true that we often use several terms interchangeably. We often refer to celebrating Mass as "celebrating the Eucharist" or "sharing in the Eucharist." We regularly say we are going to "receive the Eucharist" — that is, "go to Communion." We talk about spending time in "Eucharistic adoration" praying before the exposed "Blessed Sacrament" or in the presence of Jesus in the tabernacle. Catholics use terms like "the Real Presence" of Jesus in the Eucharist. We hear of the Eucharist as a "meal" and also as a "sacrifice." And, of course, we also talk about the Eucharist being our great act of thanksgiving, being that the actual word "Eucharist" comes from the Greek word that means just that: to give thanks. Catholics and non-Catholics alike can get confused by what all this means, and as a result, simply fail to give the Eucharist the place of honor and distinction it deserves.

To start from the top, it is important to always remember the statement I just mentioned, "The Eucharist is the source and summit of our faith." The Eucharist is the source of our faith in that it *is* Christ Himself. As Catholics, we believe that after the consecration at Mass (during the Eucharistic prayer of the priest) the bread and wine *truly* become the very Body and Blood, Soul and Divinity of Jesus Christ.

Our Lord promised us that he would be with us always, and he is in various ways. Jesus is present to us by means of the Holy Spirit who is constantly at work in our lives, even though we so often fail to recognize him. Jesus is present in our lives by means of his word. We encounter Jesus in a very real and powerful way by reading Scripture, especially the gospels. But Jesus is completely, totally, and substantially present to us by means of the Eucharist.

So we see, there are different degrees of personal presence. Think about it like this: If friends send you emails or letters, they are present to you by means of their words. They have made known to you their thoughts and communicated a particular message. If those same friends call you on the phone, they are even more present to you. On the phone, a message is being communicated, but in a more intimate and personal way in that one can hear the other's voice and distinguish a deeper sense of meaning by their inflections and expression. To take it to the next level, if friends visit you in person, they are now completely and totally present to you, body and blood, heart and soul. The same applies to our Lord when we experience his presence in the Eucharist.

So again, Jesus in the Eucharist is the source of our faith, because the Eucharist *is* Jesus himself. From that source we've been given the good news of the gospel. That very same source is that which founded and established the Church. From this source, all the other sacraments, teachings, and truths of our faith have come forth. Jesus is the source of our salvation and redemption, and all that we do as his followers should be focused on and ordered towards leading us to a deeper union with him and with each other as the "Body" of Christ. And this is where the idea of the Eucharist as the summit of our faith comes in.

After receiving Jesus in the Eucharist, we are filled with his grace and are thus empowered to go out into the world and put his words into practice. We should strive every day to live, breathe, and share the presence of Christ with others and to preach the good news of the gospel with our very lives in whatever way we are called to. Imitating Jesus is our goal, it is the summit for which we strive as we ascend the mountain of our spiritual journey. In doing this, we come to recognize how much we truly need the grace of God. We can't *be* Christ for others, unless we first *receive* Christ. And it's this realization that brings us back to that source of grace: Jesus Christ himself in the Eucharist, the most Blessed Sacrament.

THE REALITY OF JESUS IN THE EUCHARIST

LET'S TAKE A LOOK NOW at a few of those commonly asked questions. "So where do we get this idea about Jesus being truly present in the Eucharist and the consecrated bread and wine actually being the real Body and Blood of Christ?" We get this from Jesus himself. Just as we hear in the Eucharistic prayer at Mass, when Jesus was with his disciples, he took the bread, broke it, gave it to them and said, "Take this all of you and eat it, this *is* my body which will be given up for you, do this in memory of me." When supper was ended, Jesus took the cup, gave God thanks and praise, gave the cup to his disciples and said, "Take this all of you and drink it. This *is* the cup of my blood, the blood of the new and everlasting covenant. It will be shed for you and for all so that sins may be forgiven. Do this in memory of me."

These are powerful words. It's during these "words of institution," as they are called, that we believe the change from bread and wine into the Body and Blood of Christ takes place. Jesus was very direct and clear with what he said. Notice he did not say, "This *represents* my body and this *represents* my blood," or, "This *symbolizes* my body and this *symbolizes* my blood," but, "This *is* my body," and, "This *is* the cup of my blood." In the gospel of John, Jesus says, "Truly, truly, I say to you, unless you eat the flesh of the Son of man and drink his blood, you have no life in you; he who eats my flesh and drinks my blood has eternal life, and I will raise him up at the last day. For my flesh is food indeed, and my blood is drink indeed. He who eats my flesh and drinks my blood abides in me and I in him" (Jn 6:53-56). And, "The bread which I shall give for the life of the world is my flesh" (Jn 6:51).

These are hard words for many today just as they were for those in Jesus' time. The gospel of John goes on to tell us that many of those who followed Jesus could not accept this teaching and went back to their former way of life. It's important to note that here again, while some of his followers started to leave, Jesus didn't try to stop them and yell out, "Wait! I didn't *actually* mean that it's *really* my flesh and blood! Come back!" No, Jesus simply said to those who remained, "Will you leave me too?" Jesus did not compromise or speak symbolically about the nature of the Eucharist, and neither should we.

Upon hearing such scriptural references, some say, "Hold on now . . . are we a bunch of cannibals then?" The short answer is, simply, no. An interesting and quite beautiful symbol that has been used in the Church throughout the ages to explain the nature of receiving Jesus' Body and Blood in the Eucharist is that of a pelican. A mother pelican, in order to sustain her young in times of distress and need, will pierce her own breast with her beak and feed her blood to her young in order to nourish them. In a similar manner, Jesus nourishes us, his children, with his very Body and Blood to sustain and strengthen us. It is not a matter of "killing and eating Jesus" as some mistakenly believe. True cannibals (human or animal) will often kill and eat their own kind out of a sense of dominance or power. In other rare, tragic cases of humans eating (already dead) humans, it is done so out of survival and necessity and is more a matter of scavenging. Neither of these is what we do in the Eucharist.

Consider this: when we go to a restaurant and eat a double cheeseburger (or any kind of food for that matter), what happens is that the greater consumes the lesser. We, the greater, consume the food, the lesser, and it essentially becomes part of us. But when we come to Mass and receive the Eucharist, the opposite happens: we, the lesser, consume Christ, the greater. Yet, even though we appear to be *feeding on* Jesus, we are in fact being *fed by* Jesus. During the reception of Communion, the true presence of Christ in the Eucharist empowers us and floods our souls with his grace. We are nourished physically and spiritually. Our Lord thus strengthens us for our journey through life. Don't forget, you are what you eat!

It's because of this true presence of Jesus in the Eucharist that we do things such as genuflect when we come into Church. In case you forgot, a genuflection is that lunging, half-kneeling movement that gets harder as we get older. When we genuflect in church, we do so in the direction of the tabernacle. The tabernacle, as you hopefully know, is that big, ornate, metal or wood box that is in the center of the sanctuary (or possibly in another place of prominence in the front of the church or in a side chapel). The word "tabernacle" means the dwelling place of God. Inside the tabernacle are consecrated hosts, which contain the true presence of Jesus Christ. And this is why we show reverence in Church. This is why coming to Church or spending time in an "adoration chapel" where the Blessed Sacrament is present, is the greatest, most powerful place on earth to worship and pray.

I heard an interesting story once about how fascinated Mahatma Ghandi (the famous peace advocate) was with Christianity, and Catholicism more specifically. He apparently said that if he believed what Catholics do about the Eucharist, about Jesus being truly present, that he would come to Mass crawling on his belly out of humility and reverence and never leave. I don't know for fact whether or not this story is true, but it makes a relevant point. How many of us, as Catholics, don't even give the Lord any sign of acknowledgment or respect at all.

I must admit that it aggravates the tar out of me how so many Catholics come to church and don't bother genuflecting or bowing or anything upon their arrival. They simply come in, flop down in the pew and start talking to their neighbor about where they are going to go for breakfast or who won the big game last night. How quickly we forget, or perhaps just don't believe or care, that when we are in church, we are in the presence of God Almighty. It is his house, so if we are going to be talking to anybody, then talk to him! There is plenty of time later for fellowship (which is important) and idle chit-chat in a more appropriate place (like outside of church) where people are not trying to pray.

THE EUCHARIST AS MEAL AND SACRIFICE

ANOTHER FIXTURE in our churches that has great significance for our worship, and is geared toward the Eucharistic celebration, is the altar. The altar is in the center of the sanctuary in every Catholic Church and looks like a great big table. The altar has dual significance for us, just as the Eucharist has dual significance. The celebration of the Eucharist (Mass) is both a sacred meal and a sacrifice, and so the altar is both the table for that meal and also the place of sacrifice.

As we've already seen, the Eucharist was instituted at the Last Supper, and it's that supper that we celebrate and enter into at Mass. Every time we gather and the priest prays the Eucharistic prayer, echoing those same sacred words that Jesus spoke, we share in the same sacred actions that took place during that meal. As we know, we even use the same elements of bread and wine. It's in this sacred meal and in the "breaking of the bread" that we experience the presence of Christ among us and are united with him and with each other; just as a family (hopefully) is united with each other in a very special and intimate way during a meal. And just as the food that we eat during a meal gives us strength, the Eucharistic meal nourishes us both physically, but more importantly, spiritually.

It's interesting to note how important the action of "breaking bread" is in Scripture. Jesus did not just do this at the Last Supper. He used this action on several occasions to make his presence and his divine power known. He "broke bread" during the miracle of the multiplication of the loaves (see Mt 14:17-21; Mk 6:38-44; Lk 9:16-17). His disciples recognized him after the resurrection by means of the "breaking of the bread" (Lk 24:35). Jesus himself backed up the importance of these actions and of the Eucharistic meal when he *commanded* his disciples, "Do this in remembrance of me" (Lk 22:19).

The celebration of the Eucharist as a sacred meal is what many of today's Catholics seem to primarily gravitate towards. Much of our current liturgical music speaks of "sharing bread and wine," or "breaking bread," or having a "meal" together. Many of our First Holy Communion services, and even a great deal of adult catechesis today tends to focus so much on this aspect of the Eucharist that the sacrificial nature of what takes place is almost completely forgotten and overlooked. Many of our older Catholics and many popular prayers and devotions from the not-so-distant past often speak of the "sacrifice of the Mass," and it is vitally important to recognize it as such.

As I pointed out, the altar is the table that we gather around to share in the sacred Eucharistic meal, but, it is monumentally critical not to forget that it is also the place of sacrifice. The nature of an altar (even for pagan religions) is the place where things are brought before God and offered to him. In many cases, this has meant to bring about the death of something so that something else may live, be blessed, or be redeemed. The sacrifice that takes place on the altar at Mass is twofold. First and foremost is the sacrifice of Jesus himself. After the bread and wine are consecrated and become the Body and Blood of Christ, Jesus now truly present on the altar, is offered to God the Father as a *continuation* of the sacrifice of Jesus on the cross at Calvary.

An *extremely important* distinction to keep in mind here is that we *do not* re-enact, or redo Jesus' sacrifice. Jesus gave his life once and for all on the cross 2,000 years ago. We do not "crucify and kill Jesus again and again" at Mass as some non-Catholics mistakenly believe. At Mass, we enter into Jesus' sacrifice in a less graphic or "unbloody" manner. What takes place during the Eucharistic sacrifice is the *continuation* of Jesus' sacrifice as his sacrifice continues to affect us and redeem us today. The salvation offered us by his sacrifice is still present and available to humanity and it will be until the end of time. This is what we celebrate and enter into in a very real way.

If Jesus had not made the sacrifice of his life for us, if his body had not been "broken" as bread for us, if his blood had not been "poured out" like wine for us, we would have no hope of eternal life. We would truly and absolutely be doomed! And that's a fact we should not forget or take lightly! And so this ultimate act of love, the sacrifice of the Son of God on the "altar" of the cross, is what we "give thanks" to God for at the celebration of the Eucharist. This is also why purposely missing Mass on a Sunday or a Holy Day of Obligation is a mortal sin. When one consciously chooses not to attend Mass, when one purposely chooses to *not* "Do this in memory of me," one consciously rejects the salvation that Jesus won for us by means of his horrible, brutal, humiliating death on the cross.

As I mentioned, the sacrifice on the altar is twofold: the first being the continuation of the sacrifice of Jesus offered up by the priest during the Eucharistic prayer, and the second being the sacrifice that the people of God, the folks in the pews, offer up at Mass. Back in Chapter 3, I discussed that through Baptism we all share in the ministry of Jesus as "priest, prophet, and king." There is a difference between the ordained priesthood and the "priesthood of the faithful," but it is still very important to take that role seriously, to bring those "spiritual sacrifices" of our lives to Mass, to take the time to prayerfully prepare ourselves before Mass, and to consciously place those sacrifices and prayers on the altar with the Eucharistic sacrifice of the priest and ultimately, the sacrifice of Christ.

Something in our worship at Mass that is also made present in liturgical art and music, is the image or title of Jesus as the "Lamb of God." In many of our older churches and cathedrals, it's very common to see Jesus portrayed as such in stained glass windows or paintings. As we all know, before we receive Communion, we sing or recite the Lamb of God ("Lamb of God you take away the sins of the world . . . have mercy on us . . . grant us peace . . ." etc.) and immediately before the priest receives Communion himself and then distributes it to others, he holds up the consecrated bread and wine, the Body and Blood of Christ, and says, "This is the Lamb of God who takes away the sins of the world, happy are they who are called to his supper."

"So what's the deal with this lamb thing?" you may ask. Well, it's based on a reality that many would (and do) like to ignore. In the gospel of John we hear John the Baptist proclaim (in reference to Jesus), "Behold, The Lamb of God, who takes away the sin of the world." Jesus as the Lamb is also a common occurrence in the book of Revelation as we hear such things as, "You were slain, and with your blood you purchased men for God." This reference to a lamb is something that goes back to the Old Testament and was still practiced by the Jews of Jesus' time.

In the book of Exodus we hear how the blood of the Paschal (Passover) lamb saved and protected the Israelites from God's impending wrath upon the Egyptians. The lamb was slaughtered and its blood was to be sprinkled over the door of the houses where the Passover meal was taking place, and thus God "passed-over," or did not inflict his punishment of killing the firstborn of those who dwelled there. The lamb was then roasted and eaten with unleavened bread and wild lettuce (sounds pretty tasty to

Fractured and feckless

what he wants. The spending bill Congress is n

that says is halfway Democrats, and it looks ce

have no well

has years in the last two years of their secon

a "lame duck." It is because the Dems in leader

McMinnville, Oregon

me!). The parallel for us as Christians is that we believe and profess that Jesus is the one who saved humanity from eternal death by the shedding of his blood. He became the Paschal Lamb for our redemption. Jesus became for us the lamb of sacrifice in a very real way.

We also see in the Old Testament that the Jewish people participated in sin offerings as a way of atonement. As part of this custom, lambs were often used — that is, they were killed and sacrificed. The book of Leviticus gives a detailed description of this if one is interested in all the rather graphic details, but by means of killing and sacrificing a lamb in atonement for sin, one would became very aware of an important reality: Sin brings death. Sin brings destruction. Sin kills! Meditating on this reality more frequently is something that all of us would benefit greatly from. And so Jesus, along with being our Paschal Lamb who is present at the Eucharistic meal, is also the lamb that was slain in reparation for our sins. He is the Eucharistic sacrifice who truly is the "Lamb of God who takes away the sins of the world."

THE EUCHARIST AS THANKSGIVING

AT THIS POINT, I'd like to take a step in another direction for a moment and look at the Eucharist as an act of thanksgiving. Every year during the month of November we Americans get together with our families and friends, cook up a big, buttery turkey, fix all kinds of side dishes and delicious pies, and then proceed to stuff ourselves in a wild feeding frenzy like a starved Russian Boar! We engage in such societal and familial rituals as a way of expressing our thanks, although the element of true gratitude can at times get lost in a swamp of mashed potatoes and gravy, pumpkin pie, green bean casserole, cranberry sauce, stuffing, fresh baked rolls, red wine... I'll be right back, I've gotta get something to eat!

All right, where was I? Ah yes, the Eucharist as an act of thanksgiving. At the beginning of this chapter, I mentioned that the word "Eucharist" comes from the Greek word that means to give thanks. This is for good reason. At the celebration of Mass, we thank God for the greatest gift of all, which is the gift of his Son, Jesus, who purchased for us salvation. Every time we gather together for Mass, we celebrate the passion, death, and resurrection of Jesus. Every Sunday Eucharistic celebration is a continuation of the celebration of Easter morning. And again, if it were not for the sacrifice that Jesus made for us and his resurrection from the dead, we would truly be a hopeless people. We would literally be damned!

And so it is that at every Mass, and more specifically at Sunday Mass, that we not only worship our God, listen to his word, receive an abundance of his grace, enter into the continuation of the sacrifice of Jesus on the cross, and share in a sacred meal, but we do all this as a way of saying "thank you" to God with all our hearts and souls. Every Mass should have the joy, the passion, the excitement, and the devout reverence of our annual Thanksgiving holiday. Of course many of us fail to experience this, and really, there is no one to blame but ourselves (clergy included). Perhaps the following story will illustrate this point.

When I was nineteen or so, my grandmother became very ill and was hospitalized. Like any good grandson, I went to pay her a visit. After spending some quality time with her in the rather small, institutional, sterilized room, I cautiously made my way out of the hospital. Down the elevator I went, and with a fairly brisk pace I headed onward through the main corridor to the big glass doors. When I was almost there, I noticed out of the corner of my eye a little room that was jam packed with people. I peeked in, looked around, and casually asked a middle-aged man standing by the doorway, "What's going on?" He informed me that this was the chapel and Mass was about to begin. "Hey, great!" I thought to myself. It was Saturday evening, so I figured I might as well stay and get my Sunday obligation taken care of while I was there.

I shoved my way into the plethora of people and actually found a place towards the front (imagine that) to sit down, though I was uncomfortably sandwiched between a couple of gruff look-ing gals. Through a thicket of winter coats, broad shoulders, and big hair, I noticed a small makeshift altar and a little side table that had on it all the items necessary for Mass. This room was ob-viously not a permanent chapel, but simply a utility room that was probably used for all different kinds of activities.

At exactly 5:00 p.m., a well-weathered old priest, who was the full-time hospital chaplain, appeared at the door and an-nounced what number the opening hymn would be. He began singing in a loud voice as he entered the room and made his way to the altar, but there was hardly a peep out of anyone else as no one even bothered to pick up a missal or hymnal, much less even attempt to mutter along with the tune for the entrance procession. As Mass began, the priest enthusiastically recited the prayers, but the only reaction he received from those in attendance (including myself I'll admit) was a flatline, comatose, half-dead droning that sounded like a group of zombies attempting to sing a dirge. It sounded something like this: "UUrrraa goooorrr uuuuttttuaa u uu aaaoooo."

After the Gospel reading, everyone was seated and several un-easy looking folks began checking their watches to see how much longer they would have to be held as liturgical hostages. That par-ticular day was the Feast of Corpus Christi (Latin for the "Body of Christ"), and this is one of the days that we as a Church really focus intently on the nature and importance of the Eucharist. The priest began his homily by talking in a slow, deliberate, though unassuming, voice about many of the things we've looked at in this chapter already. He spoke with great historical accuracy about the origins of the Eucharist, about its significance and meaning for us, and things of that nature. Then, he paused slightly, raised his voice about five notches, got a fiery look in his eyes, gripped the portable podium as if he were driving a Mac truck off the top of Mt. Everest, and began to breathe fire as he preached, and I mean preached, about the Eucharist as an act of thanksgiving.

He laid into the unsuspecting congregation with an unforeseen might, and with tremendous intensity he inquired, "What kind of thanksgiving is it when the only reason the majority of you come to this Mass is because it's the shortest one in town!? I know that most of you here are not even visiting anyone in the hospital! You get here late, you don't sing, you don't participate in any way, you begrudgingly go through the motions like stubborn old mules, and then, you receive the greatest gift of all, our Lord himself in the Eucharist, and then just leave! You don't even stay for the end of Mass, even though it doesn't even go hardly a half an hour! You don't take even one minute to get down on your knees and thank God for what you have just received, you simply leave, still chewing on the host as you walk out the door! What on earth kind of thanksgiving is that!? You know, if you go to the grocery store and get shortchanged, you get upset, don't you? Well how do you think our Lord feels when you shortchange him week after week!?"

When the homily was finished, everyone was sitting up straight in their chairs as if they were in fifth grade and just got caught cheating on a test. You could have heard a pin drop! Everyone was suddenly wide awake and desperately fumbling through their missal to make sure they knew what to do next. No one left early that day, and the remainder of the prayers, responses, and songs at that Mass were all recited and sung with authority and great vigor. It was an experience I'll never forget, and I have no doubt that it was God's plan for me to be there that evening.

I tell that story as often as I can. It's a great way for me to rant and rave on some important points that we as Catholics desperately need to pay attention to, while doing so in the guise of someone else ranting and raving. How perfect is that? But in all seriousness, the things that priest preached on that day are things that every church-going man, woman, and child needs to hear and take to heart.

THE UNION OF COMMUNION

WELL, WE'VE COVERED A LOT of ground thus far, but there are still some important things about the Eucharist to consider. As Catholics, when we get in line and go up to receive the Body and Blood of Jesus, we call that "going to Communion" as we all know. This "Communion" is something that we often fail to see and experience the full magnitude of. I often hear Catholics say rather selfish things like, "*I'm* going to *my* Church to receive *my* Jesus, and nobody better get in *my* way or distract *me!*" We have to remember that in regards to receiving Jesus in the Eucharist, it's not just about *me* and Jesus, it's about *we* and Jesus. Obviously, receiving the Body and Blood of Jesus Christ is a very personal act, and it unites us individually with our Lord in an incredibly intimate way. When we receive Communion, we are as close to God as we will ever get during our lives here on earth. That's worth repeating. *When we receive Communion, we are as close to God as we will ever get during our lives here on earth!* That being the case, we should always spend time adequately preparing ourselves for this encounter by means of prayer and fasting. Don't forget, we are supposed to fast for at least one hour before coming to Mass and receiving the Eucharist.

Something very important to keep in mind concerning Communion, is that, again, it's not just a personal, one-on-one encounter. When we receive Jesus in the Eucharist, we are personally in union with him, but, *we* as a people, *we* as the "body" of Christ, *we* as the family of God are in union with him together, just like a family is united during a meal. We as a people become united with God during Communion.

Another aspect and reality of receiving Communion is that it is (or at least is supposed to be) a sign of our unity of faith. In receiving the Eucharist as individuals and as a community of believers, we are not only united with Jesus and with each other, but we are also expressing our unity with the entire universal Church. When we come up and receive the host and drink from the cup and say "Amen," we are saying, "Yes, I believe that this is truly Jesus, and I believe and hold all that his Church teaches." If we do not believe that Jesus is truly present in the Eucharist, if we do not believe all that he teaches us in the gospel, and if we do not hold fast to the teachings of the Church that Jesus himself established, then our "Amen" is a lie. Now I'm not talking about disagreeing with things like the way a certain bishop or pope may have handled a particular bureaucratic situation. Lord knows we all make mistakes. But if we blatantly deny any of the doctrines and the dogmas of our faith and the teaching of the Magisterium, then we are in fact not in union with Jesus and his Church; thus, we are not truly in "communion" with him.

This is why we ask that non-Catholics do not receive Communion if they are present at a Mass. It is not a matter of us trying to be mean and exclude people, it is simply a matter of expressing the reality that unfortunately we are not yet united with our brothers and sisters of other faiths. This is something that we are still working towards and hopefully one day will achieve and experience.

TRANSUBSTANTIATION AND THE EUCHARIST

AT THIS POINT, the reader may be saying, "All right, I get the message. Jesus is truly present in the Eucharist. It's very important. It's the heart and soul of our Catholic faith. It all sounds great. But come on ... I'm a grown man/woman. I'm an intelligent, reasoning, clear-thinking adult. How am I supposed to believe that a piece of bread and a cup of wine actually become the flesh and blood of the Son of God?" The answer to this question is what we call "transubstantiation."

Transubstantiation is the theological term that describes what happens to the bread and wine during the consecration as they become the Body and Blood of Jesus. It sounds pretty complicated, but it's really not. For starters, in philosophical and theological terms, all material things are made up of what we call "substance and accidents." The *substance* of a thing is essentially what a thing is. For example, the *substance* of a guitar is simply a guitar, that's what it is. It's not a rocking chair, it's not a camera; a guitar is a guitar. The *accidents* of a thing are its physical attributes: what it looks like, feels like, etc. Going with the guitar again, its *accidents* are that it's brown, it's hard, the wood has a certain feel to it, etc.

What takes place, then, during a transubstantial change is: the accidents of a thing remain the same, while the substance changes. I once did a rather graphic demonstration of this for some teenagers by taking an old guitar and smashing it to bits à la Jimi Hendrix! After I smashed the guitar apart (and it really was a piece of junk; I'd never destroy a guitar that could be salvaged), I took all the pieces and put them in a pile. After that violent episode, the accidents of the guitar remained the same: the pile of rubble was still brown, hard, and the pieces still had the same texture and feel of wood. However, the substance of the guitar had dramatically changed; it was clearly no longer a guitar. It had changed into a pile of junk! If I had had more time, I would have perhaps made something else out of the pieces of wood to demonstrate that the guitar truly became something else more substantial than a pile of junk, but they got the point.

This is what happens to the bread and wine during the consecration. Their accidents remain the same: the host still looks and tastes like bread, the wine still looks and tastes like wine, but *what* they are, their substance, has changed into the Body and Blood of Christ. Now, all this may sound good and make sense to a certain degree, but many Catholics still just don't believe it. And that is where faith comes in. If at every Mass the host physically turned into flesh and the wine physically turned into blood, I think a lot of people would be too scared to receive Communion, but if that happened, we would have absolutely no doubt at all and thus we would have no need for faith at all. And that is not how God operates. Jesus challenges us to be a people of faith. Our life on earth is about faith, and our eternal life is our reward for how we lived out that faith.

EUCHARISTIC MIRACLES

FAITH IS HARD TO DEVELOP, but thankfully our Lord gives us some help every now and again. In regards to the Eucharist, there have been many Church-approved Eucharistic miracles throughout the ages that our Lord has used to make known the reality of his true presence in the most Blessed Sacrament. Let me preface things here by saying that, as I've pointed out in a previous chapter, for the Church to approve a miracle, you can bet that the best of the devil's advocates have been involved. The Church is very, very skeptical in regard to anything miraculous. She exercises extreme prudence and caution in judging such matters and does not put her seal of approval on a miracle until every and all avenues have been explored. The Church works closely with science (who says faith and science don't mix?) and other disciplines to exhaust every possible natural explanation. As a result, when the Church finally, sometimes after decades, gives her approval, we can be absolutely sure that this is truly a miracle of God . . . so rejoice!

Of the Eucharistic miracles that have been approved by the Church, one of the most outstanding and oldest is the miracle of Lanciano, Italy, that took place around the year 700. As the story goes, there was a wise and learned priest who, like many Catholics throughout the ages, began to doubt Jesus' true presence in the Eucharist. One particular morning as he celebrated Mass, his heart was weighed down with disbelief in the words he was speaking, "This is my Body. This is my Blood." But after he spoke those words he noticed that the host visually turned into flesh, and the wine visually turned into blood in the most real manner possible. The veil was lifted, and he and those present saw the true reality of what takes place at every Mass. This was obviously a magnificent, life-altering experience for all present, and it continues to be in our present day, as the miraculous flesh and blood of that miracle are still intact and can be seen today!

A multitude of investigations have taken place over the years concerning this miracle, and in 1970-1971 (and a bit more in 1981) extensive research was done by Prof. Odoardo Linoli, who was the professor in anatomy, pathological histology, chemistry, and clinical microscopy. He was assisted by Prof. Ruggero Bertelli of the University of Siena. Their studies were carried out with absolute objective scientific precision, and they documented their studies with microscopic photographs. The conclusions of their research indicated that the host, now flesh, is real human flesh and the blood is real human blood. The flesh consisted of the muscular tissue of a human heart. Both the flesh and blood have the same blood type: AB, which is very interesting in that other approved Eucharistic miracles and the blood samples taken from the Shroud of Turin (the authenticity of which many still debate) are also type AB.

I won't bore you with all the rest of the minute scientific details — you get the point. What the priest learned that day on the altar in Lanciano, Italy, what science has backed up in that particular case, and what Jesus told us from day one is true and absolute, "This *is* my Body. This *is* my Blood." Jesus is truly "The Lamb of God who takes away the sins of the world." And how unequivocally happy we should be, for we are indeed called to His supper. So the next time you come up at Communion to receive Jesus in the Eucharist, say it loud and say it proud... *"Amen!"*

CHAPTER 6

FIRE AND FRUIT

UGO THE CAVEMAN quickened his usually sauntering pace as he began his stroll back to the safe confines of his hole-in-the-cliff home. The blazing sun was setting fast into the thick, dark clouds and all around him bloodthirsty squawks and shrill screams emitted from terrifying reptilian beasts that were beginning their evening hunt. No doubt Ugo's pungent unbathed stink was wafting through the dense prehistoric air en route to the dripping slime-filled nostrils of some awful creature with big toothy jaws and an empty gullet.

He suddenly heard thunderous footsteps approaching, and he now flat out ran for cover in a desperate fit of panic! As Ugo finally made it to the cave, he noticed a large pair of piercing red eyes peeking through the treetops at him. With a gasp of fright he scampered way back to the deepest recesses of his protective rocky lair. He huddled in the corner while deafening shrieks reverberated and echoed through the stone walls. Though scared to death, he knew he was safe, and so after his racing pulse began to slow, he settled in for another dark night in Neanderthal land.

As the last remnants of sunlight faded, his tired pupils dilated from the darkness. And so there he was once again, in the pitch black, void of all light, sitting in the terrible chocolate onyx of another caveman night. It was miserably cold. It was painfully lonely. He wondered whether it would always be so. As he tossed and turned, wrestling with the musty mammoth hide that kept him comfortable and covered from the rocky floor and the night's elements, he decided to get up and go out for a breath of fresh air.

The chaotic sounds of the evening hunt were now gone. As he stumbled around and carefully navigated his way out of the cave, a sudden blast of cool air hit his whole body. He noticed that the ambient sounds were no longer compressed by rock walls. Though the thick cloud cover snuffed out all the stars and moon and the darkness remained, he knew he was now out in the open, and safe for the time being.

While he stood outside and lethargically pondered the meaning of life, a sudden rumbling from the heavens caught his attention. Then, with a loud steely crack, a bolt of lightning momentarily lit up his dense surroundings. Again it happened, then again. As the violent canopy continued to shoot racing beams of electricity through the sky, a smile slowly eased across Ugo's face. There was light! He could see! Even though they were quick and sporadic, he was overjoyed by the comfort that came from these short bursts of illumination. Despite the frightening display from above that sent everything else that roamed throughout the land into hiding, Ugo didn't mind.

As he sat back and watched the sky's furious display, he began to ponder what he might eat for breakfast when the sun came up. Ah yes, he recalled that there was a little bit of semifresh meat on the triceratops carcass he came across yesterday. Mmmmm! Nothing quite like a mushy, chewy hunk of cool raw meat to get the digestive juices flowing first thing in the morning! With that matter settled, he drifted off to sleep.

Suddenly, an earth shattering crash and blinding light jolted Ugo from his slumber. A lightening bolt touched down not more than 25 yards away from him. Where it hit, a large tree was reduced to splinters, and coming out of the tree was a strange yellow, red, blue glow of some kind. It was on fire! Ugo curiously approached this odd sight and in a mesmerized trance, cautiously reached out to touch this bizarre, flickering thing. A puff of smoke emitted from his instantly-singed hairy hands, and Ugo snapped back his fist from the fire. It was hot! It burned him! But he also began to notice that he could see all around his immediate area. What was this strange substance? Was it a gift from the gods? He didn't know, but he was thankful for it.

As time went on, Ugo learned to be on the lookout during such storms. He began to hunt for fire. And when he found it, he'd do all he could to preserve it and keep it going. He learned to cook with it; no more putrid raw leftovers for him! Now he feasted on succulent, flame-broiled meat and potatoes! He discovered how to make torches and brighten his way at night, bring warmth to his cave, and he found friends as he brought a new way of life to those who dwelled in the outlying areas. His discovery of fire eradicated his lonely, cold, lifeless existence.

Although the hunting-gathering lifestyle provided Ugo and his (now) family and community with all they needed, abundant food, material for clothing, shelter, tools, weapons, etc., it was still hard, dangerous work. Not to mention the fact that the community was constantly on the move in search of huntable game and edible foods.

Over the years as Ugo's descendants perfected their use of fire and the lifestyle it provided, they began to discover a newer, simpler, more productive way to provide abundant food: farming.

It was found that the seeds of the plants and fruit they ate would grow more plants and fruit. After a period of experimentation, and the passing of many more decades, the Ugoites were now growing their own fruits and vegetables, which went along nicely with their protein-packed grilled dyno-pork steaks. As a local Ugo-tribe family gathered around their bright campfire one particular winter night and admired each others' smiling faces, they began reflecting on how things have changed so much and how life is now so rich, full, and abundant, all because of fire and fruit. They were a new people, and the sky was the limit as to how far they could progress. The future was bright indeed! "Thanks Great, Great, Great, Great Uncle Ugo," a youngster proclaimed!

You know, as Catholics, we too have received an abundance of spiritual fire and fruit that have the potential to dramatically improve, strengthen, nourish, and continually regenerate our lives. God has blasted us with the enlightening power of the Holy Spirit and given us an abundance of gifts to help us produce fruit in our lives, but so many of us have instead remained in the dark and failed to make use of, or even truly discover that gift, even though it has literally hit us right on the head. I'm talking, naturally, about the great gift of the sacrament of Confirmation.

JUMPING THROUGH THE HOOPS

THE UNFORTUNATE REALITY of this empowering sacrament is that far too many approach it as something they simply have to do, that they are being forced into by teachers and parents. And to tell you the truth, it was no different for me. When I was in the seventh grade, I really didn't care if I was to be confirmed or not. It just seemed like something I was supposed, and expected, to do. We spent the whole year studying about it in school. I had to do all sorts of volunteer work to rack up my required amount of service hours. I memorized virtually every prayer in the book. I had to know the "nuts and bolts" of the Catholic faith, which up until then I hadn't learned much about. Basically, I was put through a catechetical gauntlet.

After being subjected to an entire year of very intense preparation, the big day came; I was confirmed, had a pleasant reception afterwards, got some nice gifts, had my picture taken with the bishop, and then forgot all about it and moved on. Unfortunately, this phenomenon hasn't changed much for those preparing for the sacrament today. Many young people see it as simply a hoop to jump through and yet another hurdle to clear before they can go on to high school.

Even more sadly, many students see Confirmation as the official end of their religious education, and many parents see it as the finish line for providing that education. The thought is, "Okay, we've sent our son to a Catholic school; he received the sacraments, hopefully learned about the faith, and now we're finally done! The journey is ended!" And with that, many a confirmandi and his or her parents are never seen again in church until Christmas, Easter, a wedding, a funeral, or a baptism.

Of course, this isn't the way it's supposed to be. Confirmation is a new, exciting beginning in one's spiritual journey, not an end. The sacrament of Confirmation, along with Baptism and Eucharist, is one of the sacraments of initiation. These three sacraments are the foundation upon which our lives as Christians are built. We are spiritually born in Baptism, strengthened in Confirmation, and nourished in the Eucharist.

Confirmation is our own experience of Pentecost. It is where we take ownership of our faith as we "confirm" the promises made at our baptism and receive the strengthening of the Holy Sprit to go forth as living witnesses, servants, and true evangelists for Christ. Confirmation makes us soldiers for the Lord, ready to go out and do battle with the sin and evil of our culture and to bring the victory of the gospel to the world! It can be thought of as a spiritual rite of passage: "to become a man/woman" in the faith. Confirmation is the time when we're "kicked out of the nest" like a young eagle to fly on our own, to take responsibility for ourselves as members of God's Church, and to not take those responsibilities lightly. It's a time to truly dedicate and commit ourselves to being a part of our Christian/Catholic community.

THE SACRAMENT OF CONFIRMATION

CONFIRMATION HAS ITS ROOTS deep in Scripture. As the Church tells us, "In the Old Testament the prophets announced that the Spirit of the Lord would rest on the hoped-for Messiah for his saving mission." Later, in the New Testament, we hear how,

> The descent of the Holy Spirit on Jesus at his baptism by John was the sign that this was he who was to come, the Messiah, the Son of God. He was conceived of the Holy Spirit; his whole life and his whole mission are carried out in total communion with the Holy Spirit whom the Father gives him "without measure." (CCC 1286)

So, we see that from the very beginning, the Holy Sprit was at work, preparing the way for Christ, and dwelling with him during his earthly ministry. But it doesn't stop there. Jesus gave that same Holy Sprit to the apostles at Pentecost, which fired them up so that they were able to go out and proclaim the gospel and perform many mighty works for God. As we hear in the Acts of the Apostles, "When the day of Pentecost had come, they were all together in one place. And suddenly a sound came from heaven like the rush of a mighty wind, and it filled all the house where they were sitting. And there appeared to them tongues as of fire, distributed and resting on each one of them. And they were all filled with the Holy Spirit and began to speak in other tongues, as the Spirit gave them utterance" (Acts 2:1-4).

As the apostles then continued to work tirelessly and the Church began to grow, those who were baptized received that same gift of the Holy Spirit. The Church informs us that

"From that time on the apostles, in fulfillment of Christ's will, imparted to the newly baptized (by the laying on of hands) the gift of the Spirit that completes the grace of Baptism. For this reason, in the *Letter to the Hebrews*, the doctrine concerning Baptism and the laying on of hands is listed among the first elements of Christian instruction. The imposition of hands is rightly recognized by the Catholic tradition as the origin of the sacrament of Confirmation, which in a certain way perpetuates the grace of Pentecost in the Church." (CCC 1288)

As time went on, the practice of anointing with the oil of Sacred Chrism was added to the laying on of hands in order to make clear the reality of being given the gift of the Holy Spirit, and this practice has remained to our present day. This anointing with oil also highlights the name "Christian," which means "anointed" and derives from that of Christ himself whom God "anointed with the Holy Spirit."

We see in the scriptural roots of Confirmation that this sacrament was bestowed upon an individual right after Baptism. This is still the case today with those who come into the Church later in life through the Rite of Christian Initiation for Adults. When adults become Catholic and officially enter the Church, they receive all three sacraments of initiation at once: Baptism, Confirmation, and First Communion. They have spent many months studying the faith and preparing for full reception into the Church, and this is then achieved at the Easter Vigil Liturgy.

You may ask, "So why are the sacraments sort of split up and put on a time-line for everyone else?" As we saw in Chapter 3, infant/child baptism also has its roots in the early Church. And by means of infant baptism, the baby becomes a child of God, a member of the Church, and a new creation in Christ, but at this point, it is the child's parents who raise, educate, and instruct their child in the ways of the faith so that they may make the most of the abundant, life-giving grace given at baptism and grow up as a good Christian.

When the child reaches the "age of reason" and can understand and comprehend the nature of the other sacraments, it is then that he or she receives the sacraments of Reconciliation and Eucharist. And as that process of maturation continues and the child reaches adolescence, the time comes for that young person to make a personal commitment to his or her faith, to "confirm" and take ownership of that identity as a follower of Christ that was given at Baptism. As mentioned earlier, it's a rite of passage of "becoming a man," but in this case, it's "becoming a man or woman" of Christ and his Church. But keep in mind that Confirmation is certainly not a mere graduation. It's an occasion to take true ownership of one's faith and a commitment to live it out more fully.

Just as with Baptism, a candidate of Confirmation has a sponsor. The sponsor should be a person who will be, and has been, a living example of the faith, someone who will continue to pray for and guide the candidate along the right path. Also, similar to Baptism, the candidate will take a "confirmation name." This is the name of a saint that has had a special role in the candidate's life or who has been a significant inspiration. This saint is one who then can and should be looked to for heavenly assistance, prayers, and as a spiritual role model throughout one's life here on earth.

Preparation for the sacrament of Confirmation should focus on leading the candidates to a deeper, more personal relationship with Christ; a more thorough understanding of the Holy Spirit's actions, gifts, and promptings; and a greater sense of responsibility to their lives as Christians. Their preparation should also instill in them a stronger realization and awareness of the Universal

Church and a more active participation in their local parish and Catholic community.

How to successfully and fully prepare candidates for Confirmation, and all it entails, is no doubt a great challenge. As I've discussed, for many, it simply boils down to something they are being made to do by parents and teachers, and when this is the case, the result is often rebellion, a half-hearted effort, or the attitude of "jumping through the hoops" to get it over with. Personally, I feel a young person should have an authentic, genuine desire to receive the sacrament. And if that desire is not there, then I would encourage that individual to wait until it is.

If one is forced to receive the sacrament of Confirmation, the grace given and received will not be as effective as it should be due to this obstacle of a spirit of rejection. The other side of the coin is that perhaps the massive influx of grace given at Confirmation will in fact generate a renewed, divinely inspired outlook and appreciation of one's faith. This is often the case. But still, it's a tough call. The bottom line is that "you can lead a horse to water but you can't make him drink." The challenge is to gently yet inspirationally lead candidates for Confirmation to drink up that life giving water of the Holy Sprit.

THE RITE OF CONFIRMATION

LET'S LOOK NOW at the actual Rite of Confirmation. When it's celebrated separately from Baptism, as is the case usually for those who were baptized as infants/children, the Rite begins with the renewal of baptismal promises and the profession of faith. It's here that the candidates now take ownership of their faith by making good on the promises which their parents made for them years ago.

Next, the bishop extends his hands over the candidates, gesturing the outpouring of the Holy Spirit, and proclaims:

"All-powerful God, Father of our Lord Jesus Christ, by water and the Holy Spirit you freed your sons and daughters from sin and gave them new life. Send your Holy Spirit upon them to be their helper and guide. Give them the spirit of wisdom and understanding, the spirit of right judgment and courage, the spirit of knowledge and reverence. Fill them with the spirit of wonder and awe in your presence. We ask this through Christ our Lord."[13]

Following this wonderful prayer, the confirmandi come forward to be anointed on the forehead with the oil of sacred chrism. The bishop then lays his hands on the candidate's head and makes the Sign of the Cross with the oil while saying "Be sealed with the gift of the Holy Spirit."[14] A "seal," by the way, is a sign of personal authority, or ownership, and so this seal signifies that the Holy Spirit has claimed ownership of the candidate. After this, the bishop exchanges a sign of peace with the individual as a sign of unity and communion with the bishop and all the faithful. Back in the old days, the bishop would give a tap on the cheek or a "mock" slap to the face of the candidate as a sign reminding the person that he or she would have many hardships to endure throughout their life as a Christian. I think we should bring that back. A lot of these young punks could use a good slap in the face to wake them up . . . *just kidding!*

THE EFFECTS OF CONFIRMATION

WHEN THE RITE IS COMPLETE, the confirmandi then rush out into the surrounding cities, speak in all manner of "tongues," carrying on with strange wild gibberish and nonsensical gum-flapping and then perform all sorts of miraculous deeds! Right? Well, usually not. The effects of Confirmation are very real and very empowering, but they are generally less dramatic. Just as the apostles at Pentecost were given the gifts and abilities they needed to go out and fulfill their mission (like speaking in tongues), the Holy Spirit also gives us the gifts, tools, and abilities we need to fulfill our mission according to the will of God.

Just a quick word on this whole notion of "tongues." As we see in the Acts of the Apostles, this gift refers to speaking in languages that the apostles did not previously know in order to spread the gospel message. It's not necessarily babbling with strange noises that no one can understand. If no one understood the apostles or was able to interpret these "tongues," it wouldn't have done much good to spread the Good News. For us today, most of us simply do not *need* this gift; hence, we don't receive it.

The effects of Confirmation, as the Church teaches us, are:

Confirmation brings an increase and deepening of baptismal grace:
- it roots us more deeply in the divine filiation which makes us cry, "Abba! Father!";
- it unites us more firmly to Christ;
- it increases the gifts of the Holy Spirit in us;
- it renders our bond with the Church more perfect;
- it gives us a special strength of the Holy Spirit to spread and defend the faith by word and action as true witnesses of Christ, to confess the name of Christ boldly, and never to be ashamed of the Cross. (CCC 1303)

Let's examine something of great importance now and take a good look at these "Gifts of the Holy Spirit." As mentioned in the prayer of the bishop during the rite of Confirmation, the seven gifts of the Holy Spirit are:

1. Wisdom

2. Understanding
3. Right Judgment
4. Courage
5. Knowledge
6. Reverence
7. Fear of the Lord

We see reference to these gifts in Isaiah 11:1-3: "There shall come forth a shoot from the stump of Jesse, and a branch shall grow out of his roots. And the spirit of the LORD shall rest upon him, the spirit of wisdom and of understanding, the spirit of counsel and might, the spirit of knowledge and the fear of the LORD. And his delight shall be the fear of the LORD." Just a note here — the ancient Greek and Latin translations of this passage read "piety" for "fear of the LORD."

This passage from the prophet Isaiah was, of course, fulfilled in Jesus, the Messiah, "the Anointed one." And so, Jesus, anointed and filled with the Holy Spirit, embodied perfectly these gifts. As Scripture scholars point out, notice how Jesus' wisdom came through in his many parables, how his understanding was so evident in his dealings with the poor, down-trodden, and misunderstood. Notice how our Lord's courage was so strong throughout his many confrontations with the religious leaders of the day and during his passion and death. All seven gifts were present to their fullest and exemplified perfectly in Christ. All seven gifts should also be present and implemented in our lives as well. And when this happens, we see and experience how these gifts are interconnected, how they work together and flow from one another.

First, there is the gift of Wisdom. One of the initial things learned in any Philosophy 101 class is the difference between wisdom and knowledge. The basic definition of knowledge is simply to have acquired information, to have a supply of data stored in one's head like the hard drive of a computer. We human beings can know many things. It's truly amazing how much information we can collect and store in the ol' "hair covered computer." Our brains continue to sort out and gather knowledge throughout our lives, and lose some of that information as well.

As we know, some people are gifted with the ability to acquire, attain, and recall vast amounts of knowledge. There are those who are walking encyclopedias, who just have a knack for knowledge. These are the kinds of people who aced all their tests in school with no problem, perhaps without even studying. They can speak at length on any subject under the sun and go home the winner from any trivia contest or game. We often call such people "smart." At the same time, those who simply don't have the gift or capacity for billions of mental gigabytes, we often label as "dumb."

While knowledge is necessary and can certainly be exceptionally powerful when implemented in our lives, it is different from wisdom. Wisdom is the constructive and positive use of knowledge. It's interesting to note that there are folks who have little knowledge, hardly any education, yet who possess tremendous wisdom. The other side of the coin is that there are many people who are brilliant, superbly knowledgeable, but have very little wisdom. I knew a young man who got straight A's from grade school all the way through college with hardly any effort. He soaked up knowledge like a great big thirsty sponge. He could discuss business and politics with polished professionals and command great respect. But despite his stunning intellect, he was not very wise, and that lack of wisdom ruined his life.

He made the very unwise decision to start abusing drugs, to become sexually promiscuous, to get involved in all sorts of sinful debauchery and essentially toss his faith and morals into the ditch. The result was a life of destruction that hurt those closest to him, destroyed his ability to be trusted, and eventually landed him behind bars. His great ability to know was unfortunately used only to learn how to have (what he thought) was a good time. Times aren't so good for him now, and wisdom would have told him that they never were in the first place.

Wisdom, as a gift of the Holy Spirit, is that which helps us disconnect from the useless things of our culture, things that keep us from focusing on the things of heaven. It helps us to make difficult decisions based on the inspiration and grace of God. The Holy Spirit helps us to use what may seem like disastrous situations and experiences to grow in the ways of wisdom. This gift enables us to turn our faith into an X-ray vision that helps us see through the guise of false promises and sinful lies. It helps us see, know, and love the truth of God in all things and at all times.

The second gift of the Holy Spirit, Understanding, is what assists us in accepting and transforming the truth of God into eventual peace of mind. It helps us to answer those "Why?" questions that come along in our lives. Many things that happen to us, to our loved ones, to our society, to our world, we just don't know the answers to, and some we never will. But no matter what the reasons, the gift of Understanding helps us have at least a glimmer (and sometimes a truckload) of insight as to the possibilities for why these things happen. The gift of understanding also fills us with a sense of peace, with a realization that God indeed is in control and we can count on him and trust in him no matter what.

Understanding can also be thought of as common sense. The Holy Sprit sometimes just zaps us with the ability to do the right thing with no questions asked and no effort or intellectual grappling at all. There are occasions when the Spirit simply instills in us the understanding of what needs to be done, why it needs to be done, and how to do it. And thank the Lord for those great occasions of an extra helping of the gift of Understanding!

Thirdly is the gift of Right Judgment or Counsel. This gift is rooted in the virtue of prudence, which enables us to make wise decisions that help us live holy lives, avoid sin, and ultimately lead us to the salvation Christ won for us. Right Judgment is the gift that is the catalyst for the proper use of our informed conscience. When you're tempted to say something nasty about a coworker or neighbor and promptly decide not to, that's right judgment (powered by grace) at work. When your son accidentally spills milk all over the table and ruins the sports section you were so looking forward to reading, and you suddenly decide to react with prudent parental correction instead of unleashing a temper tantrum complete with a barrage of foul-mouthed enraged vocabulary, you've just exercised the gift of Right Judgment.

When someone you know is faced with a tough decision that will significantly affect his or her future in one way or another, and you find yourself able to give good, sound, inspired, and comforting advice, you've just put that gift of Counsel to proper use. When we have to vote on difficult issues, decide which candidate will genuinely be the best person for the job, and do so in a manner that is consistent with our faith in Jesus Christ and his Church, the Holy Spirit will help us make the right choice with this same gift, if we are open to using it as we should be.

The fourth gift of the Holy Spirit is Courage and/or Fortitude. These help us overcome the difficulties and obstacles that get in the way of living out and practicing our faith to the fullest. It's the spiritual muscle we need to give the devil a heavyweight fist in the face when he's trying to lure us into sin and temptation. It's the swift kick in the pants that inspires us to speak up when we should or immediately take action in a situation that needs to be addressed for the sake of Christian duty.

Courage and Fortitude help us say "no" to the glamour of evil, and they give us the strength and determination to refuse to be mastered by it. They are the gifts that the Holy Spirit gives us to exercise our true freedom as children of God, to keep us out of the slavery of sin and to bring light to our souls in times of darkness. It's no walk in the park to be a true man or woman of God. It's no easy ride to genuinely put our Catholic faith into daily practice. We can only do it with the courage and fortitude that the Holy Spirit gives us.

The fifth gift, Knowledge, is one that I spoke of generically a moment ago, but as a gift of the Holy Spirit, it's more than simply having data in our heads. When Knowledge is given by the Holy Spirit, it (as St. Thomas Aquinas would say) "perfects a person's practical reason in matters of judgment about the truth." In other words, inspired by the Holy Spirit, there are times when we just know (as well as understand) what to do in certain matters. We simply know what will be in accord with the will of God and we know right from wrong in those matters without a shadow of a doubt or without any rationalizing.

Sixth, is the gift of Piety or Reverence. This gift helps us recognize and foster a sense of the sacred, it helps us respect the reality and presence of God in things like prayer and liturgy. When one walks into a Church and identifies the presence of Christ in the tabernacle and the actuality that this is indeed the House of God, Piety is at work. During Mass, when one is made aware of the importance of participating to the fullest, Reverence is manifesting itself. This gift helps us respect more fervently things like Sacred Scripture and Sacred Tradition. It helps and motivates us to honor and pray for the leaders of our Church; and believe me, they need our prayers and support. It's a tough gig!

Piety or Reverence is the gift that reminds us to genuflect to our Eucharistic Lord before getting into the pew, to make the Sign of the Cross with passion and prayerful expression, to spend time praying before and after Mass instead of chit-chatting with our neighbor and leaving early just to be the first guy out of the parking lot. The Holy Spirit gives us this gift to draw us closer to Jesus, to enable us to experience his presence more fully in our worship, in the sacraments and in many other places. It's a gift we need to put to much more use in many of our parishes here in the USA.

Finally, the seventh gift is the gift of Fear of the Lord. Sounds a bit intimidating doesn't it? Fear of the Lord is sometimes also referred to as "Wonder and Awe in God." This is the gift that makes us aware that there is nothing worse than separating ourselves from God. To not be in God's good graces, to purposely cut ourselves off from him by a life of deliberate sin, is in fact something to be very, very fearful of. Because to do so would be to seal our fate. That's right, those who do this have sent themselves to the fiery pits of hell to roast and burn like a charred chicken leg that's been left on the grill for all eternity, while the devil stands back and laughs a pulsating mocking laugh of victory, making no attempt to put out the smoking blaze of their eternal demise! And that's putting it mildly.

God loves us more than anyone in the universe. He is almighty and all-powerful, and his majesty is far beyond our feeble human understanding. He wants us to forever dwell in his heavenly presence, but as we know, love cannot be forced. Hence, he gave us free will, that we may love him by our own accord, that we may freely choose to love him, that our love may be true and real.

God's love can and will fulfill every need or desire we could possibly think of. All the things we do in life that bring us genuine joy and lasting happiness are nothing more than subtle hints as to the joy and happiness that we'll experience in his presence in heaven. As Scripture tells us, "No eye has seen, nor ear heard, nor the heart of man conceived, what God has prepared for those who love him" (1 Cor 2:9). We can't even begin to fathom the ecstatic eternal joys of paradise that God has in store for his faithful children, and to simply throw that away as a result of our own selfish, greedy, sinful pursuits of what we think will make us happy is, again, something to have a dreadful fear of.

Another element of this gift of Fear of the Lord is the unhindered realization that God is God. He is the potter, and we are the clay. The audacity, nerve, insolence, and total disrespect we often show toward our loving Father is something else we should be extremely fearful of. How quick we forget that within the blink of an eye God could choose to not be so loving, merciful, and forgiving. Within an instant, God could unleash upon us the punishment that our culture and our world deserves. It is we who deserve to be beaten, tortured, and nailed to a cross to die in reparation for our countless offenses against God, but out of Love, it is God who took that punishment upon himself in Christ to give us another, and another, and another chance. Thank God for his merciful love, and realize and truly fear the fact that he does not have to be so.

These seven gifts of the Holy Spirit, when lived in cooperation with God's grace, authentically transform and empower us. They make us whole and bring us to completion as God's children. Just as these gifts of the Spirit changed the apostles from cowards into fearless heroes, so to it is the Spirit of God dwelling in us, given to us so abundantly at Confirmation, that can change us from sinner to saint, from a greedy, materialistic, loathsome pig of a person, to a noble, giving, selfless man or woman of Christ. As we learn to use and implement these gifts of the Holy Spirit more and more, we begin to see and experience the twelve fruits of the Holy Spirit. These twelve fruits (which are fairly self-explanatory) are: charity, joy, peace, patience, kindness, goodness, generosity, gentleness, faithfulness, modesty, self-control, and chastity.

Using the gifts of the Holy Spirit to their fullest and sharing and experiencing the fruits they produce are what lead to genuine holiness of life and a real friendship with God. Though we should have that healthy fear of the Lord and realize that God is God, that he is our loving Father, it is also important to realize that he desires to be our friend. Think about that . . . Almighty God, the master and creator of the universe, the God who was, who is, and who will always be, desires to be your closest and most intimate friend! He wants to spend time with you, to share every moment of your life, to rejoice in your happiness and comfort you in your sorrows. He's always there, searching for you, waiting for you to respond to his invitation to the great celebration of eternal love and life that he has in store for you. Why keep putting it off? Accept those gifts he has so generously given you through his Spirit, use them, develop them, let them transform you into the man or woman that God has called you to be.

It's never too late to renew your commitment to the faith and the life of grace that you took personal ownership of at your Confirmation. Sometimes it seems to take a few years for it all to set in. It did for me too. And if you haven't been confirmed yet, it's not too late to start truly preparing for the next phase of your spiritual journey. But in the meantime, let us never cease thanking God for the fire of the Holy Spirit that has brought light to the darkness of our fallen world and illumined the path that lies ahead. Let us never stop expressing our gratitude for the gifts he has so generously given us, that perhaps still wait to be unwrapped and used. Let us never ignore or detest the fruits that grow in the orchard of grace, that strengthen, purify, sanctify, and draw us to a true union with God our Almighty Father, and our best and most intimate friend. Thank you Lord, for your fire and fruit!

CHAPTER 7

WEDDING BELLS TOLL

YET ANOTHER MONDAY MORNING was upon me, and I found myself en route, as usual, to one of my favorite day-off fishing locations. I arrived at the lake around 7:00 a.m. and began to casually unload my fishing gear and get things in order. As I nonchalantly walked around the side of my vehicle, I was startled to see standing before me a huge, gigantic, absolutely enormous beast of a stray rottweiler. This dog must have weighed in at well over two hundred pounds. Its hulking, intimidating shoulders and fierce-looking demeanor was more than a bit alarming as she moved in closer to me. That dog could easily have ripped my legs off and chewed me up like a delicious breakfast burrito.

After looking her over more carefully, it appeared she was in bad shape and was certainly not going to be a threat. She was obviously very old, burned out, used up, and on her last lap. It seemed as if it took every bit of her strength to take each step as she struggled to come closer. She slowly began to sniff my shoes and look me over. She didn't have a collar or any other sort of identification, so I figured she was either dropped off by someone, or perhaps she belonged to a neighbor and simply wandered onto the property.

As I headed down to the water, she lethargically followed me. Feeling sorry for the poor old dog, I coaxed her into the water a bit to wash the caked-on dust off of her and make sure she got a drink. After cooling off she just flopped down on the bank and stared at me as I paddled off to begin fishing. As I slowly drifted away, she began to whine and tried to get up as if she wanted to come with me. Being drawn by those sad old eyes, I went back to shore and gave part of my sandwich to the noble, elderly canine. She sniffed around at my offering but didn't eat. She just kept looking at me and once again flopped back over sideways on the bank. After seeing that she appeared to be content, I made my way back out into the water.

Hours passed, and as I kept looking back to the side of the lake, there she was, just waiting for me. At one point, I thought she died as she let out an awful, long groan and rolled over on her back as if she breathed her last. Around noon, I noticed two families arrive to begin a day of fun on the water. As the kids got out of the vans, I heard bloodcurdling screams of terror as the massive black dog painfully made its way over to them. After going through the same procedure that I had earlier that morning, they too realized the dog was not going to kill them after all. It didn't take long for them to befriend each other.

As the kids and their parents set up shop on the water's edge to swim and have some good old-fashioned summer fun out in the country, the dog seemed to be overjoyed. She began swimming with the kids and paddling around the lake as best as her old legs could move her. The adults were petting her and treating her as though she was part of the family. Within a couple of hours, it appeared that the dog instantly became twenty years younger. Her old joints and bones seemed to loosen up and her tongue wagged with delight as she was the center of attention of all those laughing, gleeful kids. She knew that she mattered once again, that she had purpose and value.

That dog wasn't interested in food or water or the things that one would think she would desperately want and need to survive. What she desired more than anything else was companionship. It was evident that she had lived her life in the presence of others, that she was a part of some kind family or social unit. I'm not a dog expert, but I do know that dogs are naturally pack animals that crave interaction with others, and with her pack gone, she was alone, dejected, and down-trodden. It can be dangerous to put human emotions and characteristics on animals (anthropomorphism). We are different, and that difference needs to be realized and respected, but in human terms, that dog severely wanted to be loved.

LOVE

IT HAS BEEN SAID that love makes the world go round. Lord only knows how many songs have been written about love, how many movies focus on the trials and tribulations of it, and how many books address it in different ways. Greeting cards that contain the word "love" could be stacked to the moon. If any one of us had a penny for every time we've heard that word, there would be a lot more millionaires in the world. Everyone needs love. Young or old, big or small, we all have the innate desire to love and to be loved, and we all seek it and express it in different ways.

Love is a powerful word. Love is a dangerous word. Love is not a word to be used lightly. Love is a word filled with many connotations and possibilities. Love is nothing to play around with, ignore, or halfheartedly consider. People have killed and been killed in the name of love. Many passionate souls have gone mad or have plunged headlong into a silvery pool of self-loathing and miserable demise because of an unfulfilled longing for love, or what they thought was love. Love can inspire the truly sublime and evoke an otherworldly joy, just as it can break one's heart with a cruel twist of fate.

Oceans of tears have fallen from ecstatic, blissful eyes on wedding days, and those same eyes have gushed forth saline cascades while hunched over cold graves. A gruff old man sits in his angry chair, sipping a bitter cup while his heart drowns in loneliness. A teenage girl sobs in hopeless despair with the realization that the man of her dreams will always remain just that. A mother weeps in heavenly joy as she bathes her newborn with tender care and unbridled gratitude. One last hug and a firm handshake signal a new path while another comes to an end. Good-bye. Hello. All are occasions that are centered in love. The twang of a country steel guitar, the downtrodden yet comforting warmth of the blues, a deafening burst of symphonic perfection, and the bubblegum chewing tempo of pop music are all catalysts to express the stories of love. Blurry pages of paperback novels and emotion hijacking plots of daytime soap operas all revolve around the ways of what is perceived as love. How we love love.

Admit it or not, love is the pole and axis of our lives. After all, "God is love" (1 Jn 4:8). But love is much more than the sappy, sugar-sweet notions that many intellectually attach to it. Real love is not a mere feeling, it is a conscious decision. Love covers the gamut of emotions, personalities, occasions, and expressions. There is not one simple, universal way of defining love. It can be quite a complex phenomenon when studied as a subject in and of itself.

There are essentially three kinds of love: *eros*, *philia*, and *agape*. "Sounds like the fixin's for a fancy breakfast at one of those trendy gourmet restaurants," you may be saying to yourself. But *eros*, *philia*, and *agape* are actually Greek words that describe different forms or types of love. *Eros* is the kind of love that often initially comes to many people's minds when the word "love" is brought up. It is the (often misunderstood) expression of love that is the subject of all those songs, movies, TV shows, books, etc. *Eros* is regularly attributed to love-sick madness, crazed lustful thoughts, and overdriven desires, but in actuality, *eros* is not merely the Freudian notion of sexual, erotic love as it's thought of in today's culture. *Eros* does involve passionate, intense attraction that can lead to sexual expression, but within the framework of true love, not lust.

In his first encyclical letter, *Deus Caritas Est* (God Is Love), Pope Benedict XVI speaks beautifully and profoundly of love. He also expounds on the nature of eros love, as he points out,

> *Eros* is somehow rooted in man's very nature; Adam is a seeker, who "abandons his mother and father" in order to find woman; only together do the two represent complete humanity and become "one flesh." Second, from the standpoint of creation, *eros* directs man toward marriage, to a bond which is unique and definitive; thus, and only thus, does it fulfill its deepest purpose.

And so, in its simplest form and definition, *eros* is that which first attracts two people to enter into a deep, intimate, passionate relationship that is rooted in true love (not lust) and is later expressed physically, and ultimately, spiritually. Without *eros* love the human race would cease to exist. And make no mistake, physical attraction is a definite element of *eros* love. It's part of God's plan for a person to be physically attracted to another.

If there were no initial physical attraction (as well as intellectual and spiritual attraction) between a couple, they would not pursue a relationship. If a relationship was not pursued, their love would not grow and flourish, and thus it would not eventually reach the pinnacle of its expression in marriage and sexual intercourse. And if this sexual expression was not pleasurable, fulfilling, unifying, and life-giving, not many couples would have a desire for it. And if that were the case, there would ultimately not be any offspring, which would result in humanity negating itself.

God knew what he was doing in designing all this stuff, even though so many people have taken advantage of it and abused this great gift.

Another expression of love is *philia* love, or "brotherly" love. I hear there is a lot of it in Philadelphia! It's the kind of love shared between two friends or even more simply, the love for our fellow human being. Not too many guys I know (including me) sit around and tell their buddies how much they love them, unless they've had one too many beers! But even though many of us never, or at least rarely, say it out loud, we love our friends. Why on earth would anyone in their right mind sacrifice an entire weekend to help someone with a monumentally back-breaking task like moving if they didn't love and care about that person?

Philia love is expressed in things like having a good chat or going to a football game or on a hunting trip together. It's sharing a meal and lending a helping hand. It's offering words of encouragement and support. *Philia* love is saying hello or exchanging a quick joke. It's the outward expression of caring and giving a darn about someone else. *Philia* love can last a lifetime and age well, like a fine bottle of wine.

Swirling cigar smoke hovering over clinking poker chips and a room full of jovial laughter is *philia* love. A cooler full of longnecks, a bag of pork rinds, and the crackling of a campfire after a long day in the woods or on the water is what brotherly love is all about. It draws us together as people. It nourishes our need for companionship and human interaction. It supports us in our difficult times and rejoices with us in our victories. It comes in the form of a half-empty (or half-full, for you optimists) pizza box passed your way or an invitation to a Super Bowl party. *Philia* love is a silly email or a ridiculous phone message. It's a sense of stewardship for the good of our fellow man and a "hoorah" for all things worth living and working together for.

Last, but not least, is *agape* love. *Agape* love is the love of God. We've all heard the phrase "God is love," but so often we fail to realize exactly what that means. More than anything else, I think it's often used as a cop-out. I don't know how many times I've heard people say things like, "God is love, I love God, and God loves me, and that's all that really matters. I don't need to go to church on Sunday or go to Confession or any of that. I just need to be a good person." Errr... wrong answer, my friend!

The love of God is a self-sacrificing love. We see the ultimate expression of this love in the crucifix. Jesus, the Son of God, willing and freely suffered and gave his life out of love for sinful humanity so that we may have the possibility of eternal life and the forgiveness of our sins. He took upon himself the punishment that was meant for us because of our sinfulness and disobedience. In the crucifix we see the reality of the immensity of God's love and mercy. We see Jesus putting his own words into practice, "Greater love has no man than this, that a man lay down his life for his friends" (Jn 15:13). We are called to do the same.

We are all called to imitate the self-sacrificing love of Christ no matter what our state in life or vocation may be. This kind of love is not easy, and it doesn't always make us feel good. The call to imitate the love of God goes far, far beyond the complacency of the popular "be a good person" routine. We are all "good" people at our core. God made us, and everything God makes is good. But, as we all know, we certainly do not always do good things. The reality is that good people do evil things, and that's the nature of sin that affects us all.

The love of God is sacrificing valuable and much desired free time to lend a helping hand, perhaps to someone you may not even really like. It's going out of your way and purposely inconveniencing yourself for the good of another. It's coughing up your hard-earned cash and giving till it hurts (not just giving out of surplus) for a worthy cause. It's consciously putting yourself last so that another may be first. It's courageously striving to live a virtuous life and to keep all of God's commandments out of love, not just a sense of obligation, fear of punishment or consequence. The love of God often comes in the form of headaches and empty wallets. It's long, sleepless hours at the bedside of a sick child or spouse. It's staring into the blank eyes of the elderly who are dying from loneliness yet can't express it. The love of God is the cross and the courage to carry it. It's the willingness to die to self so that others may live.

As we've seen, there is a lot more to love than meets the eye. These three different kinds of love — *eros*, *philia*, and *agape* — are things that we all experience to varying degrees. Some focus on one form or expression more than others. As a priest, I instinctively gravitate to *agape* love. I've dedicated my life to imitating, living, and sharing *agape* love. Of course, I fail miserably at times, but it's nonetheless where I am primarily drawn. Like anyone else, I have family, friends, and people whom I care about, and so *philia* love is very important to me as well. Though I'm married to the Church, I certainly experience the attraction element present in *eros* love. I would be lying if I said I never notice a beautiful woman walking down the street and experience attraction. There would be something wrong with me if I didn't! But again, *eros* is not about lust.

True admiration of beauty is not evil. But, as we all know, crossing that line into lust can be easy. An old priest once gave me some great advice in this matter. He said, "When you see a lovely lady, don't pretend she's not there. Thank and praise God for this beautiful person, but leave it at that, in doing so you diffuse the work of the devil by turning an occasion of possible lust into a moment of glorifying God for his wonderful creation." It's good advice that has worked for me!

MARRIAGE AS THE SACRAMENT OF LOVE

THERE IS ONE VERY COMMON vocation that focuses on and embraces all three kinds of love. That vocation, of course, is marriage. So, what exactly is marriage and what is the sacrament of Marriage all about? The Church views marriage as a sacred covenant and a committed partnership between man, woman, and God. When a couple celebrates the sacrament of Marriage, they are promising a lifetime of commitment to their spouse and to God. They are promising to live out their faith in their married life together and to be active members of the Christian community.

The sacrament of Marriage is the sacred celebration of a sacred love. It is the celebration of true love. And true love is committed love. It outlasts the demeaning arguments that couples sometimes have. It goes beyond the change in physical appearance due to age, sickness, childbirth, etc. It goes beyond the financial struggles and difficulties with family and work. It outlasts the many hardships and problems that will come throughout life. The sacrament of Marriage is an experience in which the couple truly encounters (and needs) the very presence of God as they begin their new life together.

Marriage is a reflection of the love that Christ has for his Church: *agape* love. In marriage, a husband and wife promise to love each other with that self-sacrificing love of God, to focus on the good of the other, to selflessly give of themselves at all costs. The married couple becomes a source of sanctification for each other as they go through life. *Many couples overlook their ultimate goal: to get their spouse to heaven!* They should help each other stay on the right track that leads to the salvation and eternal life that Jesus has won for us. By means of the sacrament of Matrimony, couples become missionaries of God's love to each other and to the whole world. They become living witnesses of God's mercy and forgiveness.

St. Paul speaks wonderfully about the nature of love that should be shared by a married couple. But this potent and magnificent message is usually not heard due to the lack of understanding with which it is perceived. Many women I know downright hate this passage, while men think it's great. I'm sure you know the passage I'm talking about. It's Ephesians 5:21-30, and it goes like this, "Be subject to one another out of reverence for Christ. Wives, be subject to your husbands, as to the Lord." Some Bible translations, rather than saying "subject," use the stronger word "subordinate." For starters, notice St. Paul said to be subject to *one another*. And further, he said to do so out of reverence for Christ, not out of a spirit of dominance and slavery.

Now here comes that part that most people never hear because they're still so upset about that first part. Just three verses later, St. Paul states, "Husbands, love your wives, as Christ loved the church and gave himself up for her, that he might sanctify her, having cleansed her by the washing of water with the word, that he might present the church to himself in splendor, without spot or wrinkle or any such thing, that she might be holy and without blemish" (Eph 5:25-27). At the time this was written, to be told to actually "love" one's wife was revolutionary. It was without question a male-dominated society where women were often seen as property.

But the real power in this passage comes from St. Paul's directive for men to love their wives as "Christ loved the church." And how does Christ love the Church? By sacrificing his life for her! St. Paul is telling husbands to be willing and ready to be humiliated, mocked, spit upon, tortured, and put to death out of love for their wives! How about that, ladies?

In marriage, *philia* love should be present as well. Husband and wife should be the best of friends and genuinely enjoy spending time together, relishing the beauty and joys of life and supporting each other through the difficult times. Their friendship should grow and last throughout life, in good times and bad till death do they part, not just until the first big disagreement or fight arises.

Many couples tell me how difficult it is at times to keep their relationship going in the midst of the busyness of raising a family, work, etc. And just as many couples tell me of the vital importance of *making* quality time to share together, to continue to "go on dates" throughout their married life and make it a priority to keep that friendship alive. Like any thing else, it takes work.

The sacrament of marriage, of course, recognizes *eros* love, which has its fulfillment in, and leads toward, *agape* love. Most husbands and wives are husbands and wives because they were first deeply attracted to their future spouse. In married, committed love, sexual intercourse reaches the goal for which it was intended. It truly becomes the ultimate, unifying expression of physical, emotional, and spiritual love. It becomes an act of total self-giving to the other. It is an act that enables couples to become co-creators with God Almighty in bringing new life into the world. Think about that! What an incredible, awesome thing to create life out of true love! This powerful reality is obviously a very serious responsibility as well. And that is one of the reasons the Church considers sexual activity outside of marriage, and artificial contraception within marriage, a grave and serious sin.

SEXUAL MORALITY

As ANYONE WHO IS MARRIED knows, the temptation toward sexual sin does not miraculously go away with the proclamation of one's wedding vows. That temptation does not go away for priests and religious either on the day of ordination. Everybody experiences sexual temptations to varying degrees. And of all the temptations that are out there, out of all the sins that can really shatter lives, break relationships, and cause severe emotional, spiritual, and, at times, physical trauma, sexual sins would have to be at the top of the list.

Week after week, we priests hear from married people who have had an affair or have sought sexual gratification by means of visiting prostitutes, strip clubs, etc. We hear from young people who have been sexually active and are suffering the tremendous emotional pain that comes from unloving, uncaring sexual activity. We hear from people of all ages and all walks of life who are addicted to pornography and masturbation. We hear from those who are struggling with same-sex attractions, and we hear how their homosexual activity has confused and altered their sense of who they are as a human being. We hear from those who have sexually abused others or have been abused themselves. We hear from those caught up in all kinds of disturbing sexual sins. We hear from people who have contracted various diseases or who have had an abortion as the result of immoral sexual activity. And although all sin causes pain and misery, sexual sins seem to have an enslaving characteristic uniquely their own. They ruin people's lives, their self-worth, their dignity, their trust, and their hope like nothing else.

I firmly believe that one of top reasons people struggle so much with sexual sin is because of the amount of temptation that is out there these days. Not a day goes by that one is not blatantly assaulted with sexual imagery or content in one form or another. It is virtually everywhere. We see it on billboards while driving down the highway, on magazine covers at the grocery store checkout line, on radio and TV commercials, on junk email and pop-ups. Even if you're trying to avoid it and steer clear of such material, it still stares you in the face at every corner. Our culture is infatuated and truly obsessed with sex.

And the real mockery and utter foolishness is that in a world with millions of people dropping dead from AIDS and suffering from other sexually transmitted diseases, our culture thinks it's doing people a huge favor in saying things like, "Be safe, use a condom!" What a joke! Let me ask you this: if you are in a situation where having sexual intercourse is quite possibly going to give you a disease, bring a child into the world that you are not ready to take care of, or even kill you, do you really think you are doing the right thing? Are you willing to place a piece of rubber or a pill between you and your worst nightmare?

The Catholic Church gets a lot of flack these days over her teachings on sexual morality, especially those concerning things like artificial contraception and abortion. It's said that the majority of Catholics disagree with the Church's teaching on artificial contraception and many more disagree on other issues of sexual morality as well. As always, these harsh criticisms are mostly due to a severe lack of understanding on the part of the faithful and a severe lack of teaching on the part of the clergy. Many priests do not preach/teach on these issues for various reasons. Some fear the almost violent backlash that may occur when having the audacity to dare preach on some of these subjects. Some simply don't want to stir the pot and get their congregation riled up about such sensitive issues. Others don't agree themselves with the Church's stance on these things. Whatever the case may be, the word is not getting out, and the faithful are remaining blinded and paralyzed by the lack of information and proper understanding of these issues.

The Catholic Church's teachings on sexuality are wonderfully powerful and exceptionally beautiful. Volumes have been written (but not necessarily read) on this topic over the years by popes, bishops, priests, and lay men and women. There is a lot of great stuff out there, but much of this material tends to be a bit too "heady" and theological for the average person sitting in the pew who would need to take a semester's worth of classes just to understand the lingo of these documents. Thus the relevance, potency, sincere beauty, and life-altering power of these teachings gets lost in a catechetical, systematic, epistemological, ontological, metaphysical cloud of confusion.

As I mentioned a few paragraphs ago, the Church teaches that sexual intercourse is the ultimate, unifying, life-giving expression of love between a man and woman. It mirrors the total, faithful, and fruitful love that God has for all of us and that Christ has for his Church. The possibility of having a child as the natural result of sexual intercourse is something that strikes fear in the hearts of many couples. Many don't want to have children yet and others don't want any more children than they already have. Because of this, they seek ways to still be able to have intercourse yet remove the possibility of having children. Hence, the dreaded issue of contraception.

The culture in which we live in has destroyed the notion that human fertility is a sacred gift from God that *can* be managed in a healthy, holy manner and not treated like a horrible contagious disease in which one needs to take dangerous medication, use unhealthy devices, or have mutilating operations done to avoid having a child. When that happens, the life-giving, truly sacred, and unitive nature of sexual love expressed between a committed married couple is totally destroyed. And when that happens, sexual activity becomes nothing more than mutual masturbation.

The Church has always encouraged couples to use Natural Family Planning (NFP) to manage their fertility in a way that works to either avoid *or* achieve a pregnancy. When most people hear the phrase "natural family planning" they usually roll their eyes and think of it as a joke. But it's no joke. The methods of NFP that are used today (not the old rhythm method of the days of yesteryear) are equally, and in some cases more, effective than artificial contraception. NFP is a way for a couple to really learn about their fertility, to take ownership of it, to work in conjunction with it instead of destroying it and throwing it in the trash until they want to have kids. And here's the kicker, among couples who practice NFP, there is a divorce rate of less than five percent. This is because NFP fosters deeper communication between couples. It challenges the couple to find other ways of being intimate and loving toward each other — ways that are not limited to intercourse alone.

The big objection many people make to NFP is stated this way: "Who do you think you're fooling? NFP is still geared toward not having kids, which is still contraception!" In response to this, one should understand that avoiding pregnancy at certain times is a part of "responsible parenthood." Purposely cranking out as many kids as possible when a couple does not have the resources to properly care for those children is not a good thing. NFP is a way of avoiding pregnancy in a manner that still respects the sacredness of fertility, remains open to life, and is still in cooperation with God as co-creators of human life.

There are no methods of contraception that are 100 percent effective (though some are pretty close, including NFP). Barrier methods, spermicides, tubal ligation, vasectomy, birth control pills, and progestational agents all can and do fail. Not to mention the side effects of these things are horrible and in some cases can completely destroy one's fertility, eliminating the ability to ever have children. The important point in all of this, and the message that the Church is trying to get across, is to be open to life. A child is a gift from God, not the *right* of the individual. And if you are practicing responsible parenthood and still end up pregnant, then trust in the Lord. He will provide. There are lots of good resources out there for NFP. Check them out.

I highly recommend to the reader any of Christopher West's books on marriage and sexuality. Mr. West has dedicated much of his work to bringing Pope John Paul's revolutionary work, *Theology of the Body*, to the reader in a very understandable and down-to-earth style.

The nature of marriage is one of a total, unbreakable, life-long commitment, just as God's love for us is total, endless, and unbreakable. Therefore, it's not something to rush into or take lightly. It's not something to do on a romantic whim or after too much champagne while in Las Vegas. The fact that the divorce rate in America is a little over 50 percent these days is very alarming! And there are concrete reasons for this troubling rate. The most obvious reason is a lack of commitment. Many couples cannot commit and stick to it, and much of this is rooted in selfishness. The attitude of many a potential spouse is "What can I get out of it?" rather than "What can I put into it?" Remember, the covenant of marriage is rooted in self-sacrificing, selfless love, in good times and in bad times (no matter how bad), until nothing but death separates and ends that marital bond.

PREPARING FOR MARRIAGE BACKWARDS

MANY COUPLES SHOOT THEMSELVES in the foot from the get-go by preparing for marriage in a backwards fashion. The routine for more and more couples these days (including so-called Catholic couples) goes something like this: they become sexually active (and in some cases have children), they move in and live together, they finally get engaged, they make reservations for the reception hall and DJ, book the limo service, plan the meal, pick out a nice wedding cake, get the invitations going, pick out a church they think will make a pretty backdrop, and then contact a priest to do the wedding and any of the marriage prep they'll have to suffer through to be able to have a "church wedding."

The sad reality of many (most, in my experience) Catholic weddings is that the couple has not been coming to Church, has no intention of doing so, does not support the Church in any way, does not take their faith or anything about the Church's teaching seriously, and does not pray or make any attempt to nourish their faith together as a couple, and they live lives that directly contradict everything that a Catholic couple should be striving for, most importantly that self-sacrificing, life-giving love of Christ. Yet when a priest challenges them on these things (if they even do) and requires certain commitments before he agrees to do the wedding, the couple gets insulted and often "leaves the Church" (which they've actually done years ago anyway), and the bride-to-be then has her mother call and harass the priest for being such an obstinate jerk.

In dealing with such couples, I try to explain to them the actuality of things. When a couple is living together, essentially as "man and wife," it completely destroys the authenticity of what a Catholic sacramental wedding liturgy is all about. A wedding is an expression of the reality that these two individuals are being united as "one flesh" and are from that day, from that moment, going forth to live as a household, as man and wife. If that reality is not there, the whole thing becomes a lie and a fantasy. Catholic liturgy is not about putting on a nice show. Everything has meaning and is done for a reason: to express truth. And if that truth is not there, it becomes a mockery and even a sacrilege, which I, for one, will not and cannot, in good conscience, be a part of.

PREPARING FOR A "CHURCH" WEDDING

THE REALITY AND TRUTH of what a couple is entering into by means of the sacrament of Matrimony is also why a wedding should take place inside the church and not outdoors or at another location. In a Catholic marriage, the couple is promising to live out their Catholic faith within their lives together and also within the Christian/Catholic community at large. As we've seen, they are pledging to mirror the love Christ has for all his people: the Church.

This being the case, the bestowal of the sacrament is never considered an exclusively "private" experience. It is rather something that the whole Church rejoices in and is invited to participate in. Thus, because a church is the official house of worship for all God's people and the dwelling place of Christ himself (in his Eucharistic presence), it's expected that the sacrament be administered there. The sacraments of Baptism, Confirmation, and Holy Orders take place in the Church for essentially the same reasons — it is not just a personal commitment, but one to Christ and the Church he established, so again, it naturally follows that these things take place where he is most truly present and where all the people of God regularly gather.

The sacrament of Marriage is a real bestowal and experience of God's powerful grace, a grace that strengthens the couple's love and commitment. Like any of the sacraments, it is something to prepare for, to fully understand. Children (or adults) preparing to receive the sacraments of Reconciliation, Eucharist and Confirmation spend the better part of a year studying the nature and implications of the sacrament and growing spiritually for the proper reception of those sacraments.

Those preparing to receive the sacrament of Holy Orders spend numerous years getting ready. Yet many of the would-be faithful simply expect a priest to turn a blind eye to the fact that a couple is living a life in total contradiction of the nature of the sacrament of Matrimony, that they are doing virtually nothing to grow spiritually or to truly understand what it is they are preparing for, and they simply expect the priest to do their bidding and succumb to their ceremonial demands.

Many couples huff and get upset when they find out they have to meet with a priest several times and attend various marriage classes or workshops. And herein lies the major problem, and in my opinion, one of the greatest causes for divorce: couples are not properly prepared for marriage. Many of them spend all their time preparing for a *wedding*, but not necessarily for a *marriage*. The mantra that I adopted from a seminary professor, who adopted it from the Engaged Encounter movement, is that a "Wedding lasts less than an hour, a marriage is to last a lifetime." (By the way, I can't say enough about how enriching and transforming Engaged Encounter weekends are for couples preparing for marriage. Check it out!)

One of the first things that most couples want to know when I meet with them is all the details of their wedding ceremony. They sometimes get aggravated when I tell them that that is the absolute last of our concerns and will therefore be the last thing we focus on. I always tell couples that they should quadruple their time, attention, and effort in focusing on their future marriage and not on all the details of the wedding ceremony.

They need to put everything on the table in regard to their relationship for a brutally honest dissection, analysis, and for serious consideration. *All* of those old skeletons should be pulled out of the closet. *All* of those worst-case scenarios they fear discussing and even thinking about must be brought to light. *All* of those things they think would never happen must be looked at. *All* the questions of "What if ...?" should be applied to virtually everything conceivable that concerns their relationship and future marriage. A couple must be prepared for everything and anything in their marriage. They must know how the other will react and how they feel about things. Those things have to be looked at and dealt with long before they say "I do" and worry themselves to death over having birdseed or bubbles at the end of the wedding.

As I already mentioned, in my opinion, it's this major lack of preparation that is responsible for divorce. Couples are going into marriage hyped-up on all the "wedding bliss" articles they read in their favorite magazines or hear at "Bridal Extravaganzas" while having no idea of the demands, sacrifices, and real commitments that come with marriage.

Many couples believe and argue that living together before marriage is a good way to prepare themselves. But what they don't realize or know is that current studies have indicated that cohabiting before marriage increases the risk for divorce by another 46 percent on top of the already 50 percent! Living together outside marriage also increases the risk of domestic violence for women and the risk of physical and sexual abuse for children. One study found that the risk of domestic violence for women in cohabiting relationships was double that in married relationships; the risk is even greater for child abuse.[15]

The couple who lives together before marriage is essentially training themselves for a life of noncommitment. Within the structure of cohabitation, the couple knows that if any troubles arise, they can go their separate ways without the mess of divorce. That being the case, there is absolutely nothing keeping them together except for their own desire and often selfishness. There is nothing like a marriage vow to concretize a commitment. When couples cohabit for a long period of time before marriage, this mind-set carries over into their marital relationship, and when those troubles, arguments, disagreements, and challenges of married life come, they simply split. As stated in the previous paragraph, the statistics concerning cohabiting couples who later married speak for themselves.

Over the years, I've heard from couples who lived together before marriage and those who did not, and their comments are universally the same. The couples who lived together before marriage all say, "The wedding was great, the honeymoon was spectacular, but when we got back home and all the excitement faded away, it was business as usual. We were in the same house, the same living situation, the same routine. There was no sense of truly beginning a new life together." On the other hand, the couples who did not cohabit before their marriage all tell me this: "The wedding was great, the honeymoon was spectacular, and when we came home and all the excitement faded, there was a whole new phase of excitement as we began a brand new phase of our relationship, as we began living as husband and wife truly committed to each other and to God." And this is what the sacrament of Matrimony is all about — expressing the beauty and (what should be) the reality of this new life, this sacred covenant between man, woman, and the Lord.

SAME-SEX MARRIAGE?

TO SHIFT GEARS A BIT now, another big current issue concerning matrimony is the issue of gay marriage. Before we consider the validity of homosexuals receiving the sacrament of Matrimony, it would first be good to look at the issue of homosexuality itself. The "gay lifestyle" is promoted and being "celebrated" with great enthusiasm in our culture today. There are TV shows, mainstream magazines, radio programs, and even entire media networks that cater to and revolve around homosexuals. Of course many in our society see this as a great social advancement and a huge leap forward for diversity and acceptance for gays. Meanwhile, anyone who says or thinks otherwise is aggressively labeled as an ultra-conservative, closed-minded, backwards, homophobic monster.

The common arguments we hear are: "Homosexuality is natural; people are born with that inclination. Individuals have a right to live how they choose and love who they want. Politics and religion should not restrict two loving adults from entering into a marital union. Science proves homosexuality is not a disorder," etc.

For starters, there are lots of scientific and psychological studies on the causes of homosexuality, and none of them as of yet is conclusive. Homosexuality may be caused by some biological factors, or it may be caused by social conditioning such as growing up in a dysfunctional household with improper role models or negative experiences with persons of the opposite sex. In some cases, people are seduced and coerced into the gay lifestyle; and in other cases, it is freely chosen as an "alternative lifestyle" by the persons themselves. Some say, "Why would someone choose to be gay and take on all the trouble that comes with that lifestyle?" I don't know the answer to that question, but from my experience of hearing Confessions, I can soundly verify that this is, in fact, the case with many homosexuals. There are studies out there that will back up any argument one attempts to make regarding issues concerning homosexuality. That being the case, I'll limit my comments to common sense, objective truth, and the Word of God.

First of all, the Church does not teach that "God hates gays" or that people of the same sex can't have a loving, committed relationship. The issue is how that "love" is expressed. (I'm going to get a bit graphic here, so be prepared). The bottom line, which nobody wants to face and hear, is this: Homosexual acts ("expressions of love") such as anal and oral sex are *not* natural. They are by means of their very definition gravely, objectively disordered. Those body parts were not made to go together, and when they are forced, terrible things happen. It's as simple as a basic plumbing lesson.

These acts are not *naturally* unitive and again they do not foster life. As we've seen, the ultimate expression of committed love (sexual intercourse) between a man and a woman not only unites the couple physically, emotionally, and spiritually, it not only brings life and fulfillment to the couple, but it is biologically ordered to bring about new life. Think about that. An act of love having the power to bring new life into the world! Awesome! Now, how can one possibly compare that with two people of the same sex engaging in things such as anal sex? Absurd! Such unnatural acts only bring about pain, death, and disease. The same applies to heterosexuals engaging in these acts.

The homosexual lifestyle (and, yes, the promiscuous heterosexual lifestyle) is self-negating. In reality, it is a not a *lifestyle* at all, but rather a "deathstyle." The millions dying from AIDS and other diseases give clear witness to this. When one has to use multiple forms of "protection" while engaging in sexual activity, when there is the real threat of death and disease, it should be clear that it's not a good idea to be engaging in such an act in the first place. It's sheer madness!

Contrary to public opinion, the Church is not a group of homophobic old men trying to make life miserable for people who struggle with same-sex attraction (which is the essence of homosexuality). In fact, there are programs and organizations in place that minister with those struggling with same-sex attractions. One such group is Courage (www.couragerc.net) and another is Exodus International (www.exodus-international.org).

The Church's message is to not let our culture label one as "gay" and thus encourage all the negative attributes identified with it. When that happens, all hope is removed. Just as with same-sex attractions, there are those who are *born* with a disposition toward violence, extreme aggression, depression, etc. A psychotic killer acts in accordance with his "natural" thought processes and desires. Is this a good thing that should be encouraged? No.

There are those who are *conditioned*, by means of their environment and upbringing, to use drugs and alcohol abusively. Should this abuse be celebrated with parades? No. There are those who *choose* to live a life of crime. Should it simply be ignored and thought of as an alternate way of living? No. It would be like telling someone who's trying to quite smoking, "You're a smoker. You'll never be able to give it up or live a healthy life, so go ahead and smoke yourself into oblivion." Or, like saying to an alcoholic, "Well, you have been born with an unstoppable craving for alcohol; and that's simply a part of who you are, so drink up!"

The point is this: it really doesn't matter if a disorder is either present at birth, conditioned, or chosen. It remains a disorder. It is not justified by cause. And again, homosexual sex, by its objective definition and nature, is gravely disordered.

So what does God have to say on the issue? The Bible is quite clear about the will of God concerning both marriage and homosexuality. In the book of Leviticus, we hear that it is an abomination for a man to lie with another man as he would with a woman (see Lev 18:22 and 20:13). Of course, the same law would apply to a woman. In the letter of St. Paul to the Romans, we hear: "Claiming to be wise, they became fools, and exchanged the glory of the immortal God for images resembling mortal man. . . . Therefore God gave them up in the lusts of their hearts to impurity, to the dishonoring of their bodies among themselves, because they exchanged the truth about God for a lie and worshipped and served the creature rather than the creator, who is blessed forever. Amen. For this reason God gave them up to dishonorable passions. Their women exchanged natural relations for unnatural, and the men likewise gave up natural relations with women and were consumed with passion for one another, men committing shameless acts with men and receiving in their own persons the due penalty for their error" (Rom 1:22-27). Need I go further? (By the way, a book I highly recommend on moral theology concerning homosexuality is *The Truth about Homosexuality*, by John F. Harvey, Ignatius Press, 1996.)

What, then, does God say of marriage? In Genesis we hear, "God created man in his own image, in the image of God he created him; male and female he created them. And God blessed them, and God said to them, "Be fruitful and multiply, and fill the earth and subdue it" (Gen 1:27-28). In the gospel of Mathew, we hear Jesus say (regarding marriage): "Have you not read that he who made them from the beginning made them male and female, and said, 'For this reason a man shall leave his father and mother and be joined to his wife, and the two shall become one'? So they are no longer two but one. What therefore God has joined together, let no man put asunder" (Mt 19:4-6).

And so we see that God created man and woman, not man and man or woman and woman, to be united to the point of becoming one flesh in marriage. The very nature and design of the male and female body gives clear, obvious, undeniable witness to this as well: the two are designed to go together, to be unified and bring about life.

Scripture informs us that it is God's will for man and woman to enter into the sacred covenant of Matrimony. It is God's will for husband and wife to be a source of life and sanctification for each other, and it is God's will that they bring children into the world, if they are able.

Many ask, "What about couples who marry later in life or couples who can't have children? Is the validity and sanctity of marriage only based on the ability to procreate?" The answer to this question is no. A couple who can't have children are still a part of God's plan in that they are united in love, have become one flesh, and that their sexual expression is still a truly unitive, sacred, *naturally* ordered act.

Another question is, "What would be wrong with a homosexual marriage, then, if God and religion was taken out of the picture?" To answer that, I simply pose another question in response: "What would be wrong with anything evil and disordered if God were taken out of the picture? It is God who gives us his commandments and his directives out of love to keep us from destroying ourselves, our communities, and our world." When we push God and all that is good out of the picture, we welcome all that is not good and thus we embrace evil. "Each tree is known by its own fruit" (Lk 6:44), our Lord tells us. Many of the trees we have planted in our current time have been fertilized by lies and corruption. The seeds were sown by the evil one, and the fruit they bear, which our culture feasts upon, has poisoned us and only nourished our desire for that which is vile and brings death.

THE VOCATION OF PARENT

A SECONDARY VOCATION, that in most cases naturally comes along with being a husband and wife, is being a father and mother. As we've already seen, the institution of marriage, by means of conjugal love, is ordered to bring new life into the world and hence establish a family. The family is the backbone of society. Within a healthy family unit, the parents are supported and nourished by their love for each other, and they can thus be a source of support for their children. The family structure should create discipline, respect, and love and instill virtue, integrity, and commitment for all its members.

It is out of love that parents don't take the easy way out in raising a family, and they garner the courage to work through difficult times. It's out of love that parents say "no" to their kids when need be, that they don't compromise in teaching right from wrong. Sadly, this approach is greatly lacking. We see it when parents give their teenage daughters birth control pills and their sons condoms instead of teaching true responsibility and moral integrity. We see it when parents simply put their child on more medication and send them to therapy (which is obviously needed in some cases) instead of replacing permissiveness with true, loving, parental discipline.

When the healthy family structure crumbles and that backbone breaks, the result manifests itself in carelessness, disrespect, hatred, vice, irresponsibility, and a severe lack of commitment. It evokes and fosters social disarray, and Lord knows we have enough of that already!

The vocation of being a parent is naturally one that should not be taken lightly or halfheartedly. It's also of the utmost importance to remember that to have a child is not the *right* of an individual, but a *gift* from God. The future of our world in many regards depends on parents doing their job to raise good, responsible, faithful children and guiding them to become good, responsible, faithful adults who will one day be running our country and our entire world for that matter.

HOMOSEXUAL PARENTS?

THE ISSUE OF PARENTING is also one that is under attack and is being pressured by gay advocates. Many homosexual couples not only want to have their union be legally recognized as a "marriage," but they also want and expect the "right" to have children. Homosexual sex is obviously not ordered to bring life into the world, making it an objectively disordered act, yet homosexual couples seek to adopt, find a surrogate mother, or seek out artificial means of having children.

Think about that for a moment: To have a human egg, which may not even be the mother's, fertilized by the sperm of a man who very well may not have any connection whatsoever (certainly not one of true love and commitment) to the mother as the method for bringing about a new life is as far removed from God's plan as one can get. Similar methods are just as far removed. It is the most selfish, mocking act that could ever be carried out. It is a covetous, self-centered, self-indulgent, act that completely and consciously shuts out and removes the author of life (God) in the most aggressive manner possible.

Bringing a child into the world in this manner is on a lower level than going to the pet store to pick out a new dog! It's like going out and spending thousands of dollars on Christmas presents all for one's self. Life is a precious gift given by God Almighty; no one has the right to rip that gift away from the giver and steal and tear it asunder for one's self. The bottom line is that artificial fertilization treats a child as a product, as a mere thing, rather than as a gift from God.

As mentioned earlier, many homosexual couples seek to become parents by means of adoption instead of artificially having children. Adoption is indubitably a wonderful thing. God only knows how many children are abandoned, neglected, or simply not wanted. For responsible, loving adults to welcome a child into their lives and become that child's caretaker, guardian, and ultimately foster parents is a truly beautiful act of charity and self-sacrificing love. After all, St. Joseph was a foster parent! So the question is asked, "Why can't a responsible, loving homosexual couple be adoptive parents?"

There has been a great deal of "research" stating that homosexual parents do just as fine of a job raising children as heterosexual parents. However, in an article by Glenn T. Stanton[16] entitled *Examining the Research on Homosexual Parenting*, we see that this is not necessarily the case. Mr. Stanton states, "Contrary to what the American Academy of Pediatrics claims, the research comparing outcomes from homosexual parenting and heterosexual parenting are notoriously inconclusive. There is a larger body of scientific literature showing children need a mother and father for proper socialization." A few points that Stanton offers for consideration are the following:

- Drs. Robert Lerner and Althea Nagai, professionals in the field of quantitative analysis, conducted a study for the Marriage Law Project looking at forty-nine empirical studies on same-sex parenting. The title of their study, "No Basis," is their conclusion, for they find no basis for the conclusion that children raised by homosexual parents look just like those raised by heterosexual parents. Why? As Lerner and Nagai explain, "The studies on which such claims are based are all gravely deficient." They found at least one fatal research flaw in each of the studies examined. The primary problem they found was the use of very small and unrepresentative study samples, with missing or inadequate comparison groups. In addition, most of the research subjects volunteered for the studies, and some participants were allowed to recruit other participants. Each of the authors of these studies, with one exception, wishes to influence public policy in support of homosexual families. Lerner and Nagai conclude, "For these reasons, the studies are no basis for good science or good public policy."

- Another recent study in the *Journal of Marriage and the Family*, analyzing the current research on homosexual parenting, finds "a persistent limitation of these studies, however, is that most rely on small samples of White, middle-class, previously married lesbians and their children. As a result, we cannot be confident concerning the generalizability of many of the findings."

- *The American Sociological Review* explains that it is currently "impossible to fully distinguish the impact of parent's sexual orientation on a child" because most homosexual child-rearing homes didn't start out fresh from birth, but are clouded by the dynamics of divorce, remating, and stepparenting issues that are problematic in themselves and separate from issues related to gender of the parents. Though the authors of this study are sympathetic with homosexual parenting, they "disagree with those who claim that there are no differences between the children of heterosexual parents and children of *lesbigay* parents." They indicate that problems of gender identity and sexuality might be greater for children raised by homosexual parents than any of the studies recognizes.

- Specifically, the *American Sociological Review* study reports 64 percent of young adults raised by lesbian mothers reported considering having same-sex relationships. Only 17 percent of young adults in heterosexual families reported the same thing.

- The American Academy of Pediatrics even admits in its own report that "the small and non-representative samples studied and the relatively young age of children suggest some reserve." But they ignore their own caution and state that everything works out great for children raised by homosexual parents.

As Stanton concludes, "There is an absolute mountain of social science research showing that children who are raised with their married mother and father do far better in every measure of well-being than children who grow up in any other family situation. Rarely is the social science literature as conclusive as it is on this point."

With all this being said, I'll still be the first to say that as with almost any topic based on "scientific research," one can come to any conclusion one desires if he or she looks around hard enough. Again, there have been "studies" done that will back up practically any proposition one may make. If I searched the annals of time and space with relentless devotion, I could probably find a study that scientifically "proves" that the moon is, in fact, made out of cheese, and that the earth is flat after all!

When it's all said and done, and we go round and around with research, studies, and intellectual warfare, what still stands strong and tall and remains unchanged is the truth of God. The truth is that God created man and woman for a specific reason. The truth is that only a man and woman can *naturally* bring a child into the world with the grace and gift of God. The truth is that a child needs his or her parents, and those parents also need each other. Parents need to be loving, committed, mature, and faithful if they are going to be successful in their role as parents. When any of these divinely engineered factors is missing, things being to fall apart. When a child is brought into the world by parents who do not have a loving, committed, mature, faithful relationship, rooted and concretized in the sacred covenant of Holy Matrimony, the chances of that child growing up in a dysfunctional environment are greatly increased.

We all know good and well that there is no such thing as the perfect family. Everyone fails, sins, and falls short of living up to the vocation that God has called them to or the role they are currently in as part of a family unit. Parents argue and fight. Children disobey their parents. Divorce, separation, abuse, and a multitude of other evils can work their way into any relationship. And yes, in the fallout of those situations, children can still be raised with care and love by heroic single parents and adoptive parents, but the simple fact remains that this is not how God intended it.

Our Lord did not intend for children to be abandoned and neglected, thus creating a need for adoption. Our Lord did not intend for couples to have children out of wedlock where there is no commitment and no true family structure in place. It is not God's will for one parent to leave the other, thus forcing the other to struggle like heck to make ends meet and take care of their children alone. It is certainly not God's will for a child to be produced and manufactured by artificial means like a custom stereo system for a greedy consumer.

As always, it is sin that is at the root of abuse, abandonment, divorce, separation, and all the things that destroy and degrade the vocation of marriage and that of parenthood. It is sin that rips out the spine of the divinely created institution of the family. Without God in the picture, it wouldn't matter who got "married" or became parents, and it would make no difference by what means one became a "parent." When the truth of God is flushed down the toilet of "enlightenment and social advancement," we might as well hand over our children to a bunch of apes to be raised like Tarzan.

When we shut out the truth of God, we live a lie, and those lies make us into the greatest fools that ever walked the earth. Without God, wedding bells no longer mark the beginning of a sacred vocation that gives way to the building up of the family and ultimately the Kingdom of God, but they instead toll a dreaded, somber tone that marks the beginning of the end, and the execution of true life and love.

CHAPTER 8

THE CALL

A QUESTION WE PRIESTS get asked quite often, especially us younger ones, is, "So what made you decide to become a priest?" People are very curious as to why in the world a seemingly normal, healthy young man would want to give his life to the Church, make a promise of celibacy and obedience, and spend the rest of his days in service of God and his people. Doing such a thing sounds like a nice and noble idea to many folks, but when one actually takes the religious vocation plunge, there is often shock, fear, and even contempt on the part of others.

I don't know how many times I've heard very pious, devoted Catholics say things like, "Oh, it would be so wonderful if Johnny would become a priest, he's such a nice boy, his mother would be so proud." But when Johnny grows up and actually decides to pursue the priesthood, the reaction is, "Has he lost his mind? He's such a handsome young man, he could easily find a wife. He's so talented and smart, he could really go places. He could pursue any career he wanted. What a waste! What must his parents and friends think? Is he gay? Surely there is something wrong with him! He must be hiding from something to want to become a priest of all things! My, my, my, such a shame!"

It's been noted by vocation directors across the country that the biggest deterrent to young men and women entering religious life, or even considering such a vocation, is their parents. Many are simply convinced that to be a priest, nun, monk, etc., means to live a lonely miserable life surrounded by misfits and weirdoes who couldn't hack it in the real world. Parents don't want their children to live a life of professed poverty or spend all their days in a secluded community wearing drab clothing. They don't want their sons under the thumb of some "ill-intentioned" bishop or their daughters having to subject themselves to serving those in low places, riddled with sickness, laboring with menial work, and not getting paid a dime to do such. There are loads and loads of false stereotypes out there about those in religious communities and about priests. Well, let me just say this, if the priesthood was as full of homosexual child molesting fiends and villains as the media would have us believe, I sure as heck would not be one!

The reasons that young (and older) men and women enter the priesthood and religious life are quite diverse. Every priest, religious sister or brother, and seminarian I know has a unique story as to how they were called to that vocation. The days of a young man going to a Catholic grade school, then to a high school seminary (a "prep-school") and finally on to a college and graduate school seminary in preparation for the priesthood are all but gone for the most part. The days of the "lifers" have vanished, with rare exceptions.

Most men entering the seminary these days are coming in after attending a "regular" high school, or even more common today, during their college years or even later in life after having been working in a different field for many years. I know priests who were lawyers, doctors, military men, tradesmen, artists, musicians, engineers, salesmen, factory workers, you name it. God calls people from all walks of life, at different stages in life, from very different backgrounds, and with very different abilities to follow and serve him and the Church. It was no different from day one.

JESUS CHOSE TWELVE ORDINARY GUYS

IN THE PASSAGES OF SCRIPTURE that tell us of Jesus choosing and commissioning his twelve apostles, we hear that he had many followers; some stayed and some went. But out of all those people who followed Jesus, he specifically choose twelve to be his apostles to learn from him and to eventually carry on the mission and spread his message throughout the world.

For such an enormous task and responsibility one would think that Jesus would have chosen the smartest, wisest, most courageous, most elite twelve people on the face of the earth. One would think that Jesus, the Son of God, would have picked out twelve of the holiest, most charismatic, most determined, most organized and disciplined people in the world. One would think that the twelve people that Jesus would have chosen to be his divine crew would be the twelve Godliest people that ever lived. But ironically, this was not at all the case initially.

The twelve that Jesus chose did not have great power or wealth or superintelligence. They did not have tremendous courage or wisdom or fortitude. They were not known for being the holiest of people. The twelve apostles were regular guys from all walks of life. They were twelve ordinary men, who with the grace of God and the power of the Holy Spirit, were able to do extraordinary things for Christ and the Church.

Peter, who would become the first pope and was the "rock" upon which Jesus built his Church, is the same man who denied Jesus three times in his hour of need, who when meeting Jesus for the first time said, "Depart from me, for I am a sinful man." Peter, along with James, John, and Andrew where fisherman, and they were the first chosen by our Lord.

Matthew, as we know from gospel accounts, was a tax collector. Tax collectors of that time were basically professional crooks.

They were hated by all. Tax collectors were notorious for overtaxing people and becoming quite wealthy as a result. Simon was a zealot. Zealots were known to be crazed political activists who incited all sorts of violence and uprisings. Judas ended up betraying Jesus and handed him over to be put to death. Thomas, despite all he witnessed and experienced while accompanying Jesus, had no faith whatsoever and simply would not believe that Jesus rose from the dead until he was able to see Jesus for himself and personally examine his wounds. All of the people Jesus chose then to be his apostles had many faults and failings. And likewise all those Jesus chooses today have faults and failings.

But in the midst of their sinfulness and their many imperfections, the twelve all had one thing in common: they were *willing* to follow the Lord. They were willing to do his work. They were willing to allow the Lord to work through their ordinariness to do extraordinary things. And it was through these twelve ordinary, imperfect people that Jesus built his Church that we are all a part of today, 2,000 years later.

When we look back through history, and even at current events, it truly is a miracle of God that the Church has survived all these years. Over these 2,000 years, there have been lots of people who have made lots of mistakes and who have caused a lot of damage to the Body of Christ (the Church) in lots of different ways. As I pointed out in Chapter 1, I run into people all the time who have abandoned the Church and, in some cases, even abandoned their faith because a priest or a nun or someone said something that made them mad years ago, or because they disagree with the decisions a bishop has made, or because someone at church gave them a dirty look, or whatever else. The excuses are endless.

It's very easy to find imperfections in others and to point the finger at the mistakes that those in positions of leadership have made. It's very easy to find traits in others that anger us and enrage us. And if that's what we're constantly on the lookout for, if sinfulness, faults, and failings are what our faith is dependent upon, all we need to do is have a good hard look in the mirror. There we'll see all kinds of faults and failings.

Jesus very easily could have identified a multitude of imperfections in his followers. He can identify a multitude of imperfections in each and every one of us. He could have chosen twelve of the holiest, most perfect people that ever lived to be his apostles. But he saw in those twelve what he hopefully sees in each one of us. He saw people who, in the midst of their sinfulness, still wanted to live holy lives as best they could and thus truly strived for that holiness.

Jesus saw people who, in the midst of their many mistakes, wanted to be forgiven. He saw people who needed his love and who were willing to share that love with others. He saw people who, in the confines of their ordinariness, wanted to do extraordinary things for God. And it was their faithfulness and it is our faithfulness that allows God to do extraordinary things each and every day.

In this sense, all followers of Christ — all Catholics as well as Christians of other denominations — are, by means of Baptism, called and given the vocation to be disciples and apostles. We all are called to share in the life and ministry of Christ. There is, however, a distinction to keep in mind between a disciple and an apostle. A disciple is one who follows and learns from a master. An apostle, on the other hand, is one who then takes what is learned and goes out to teach others and to carry on a mission. Although we are all called to follow and learn from Jesus, and to evangelize to others, those answering the call to a religious vocation are called to a specific mission and a more particular way of living out their baptismal vocation and calling.

RELIGIOUS VOCATIONS AND THE SACRAMENT
OF HOLY ORDERS

AT THIS POINT, it would be good to define our vocational terms. You may be asking, "So what exactly is the difference between things like a diocesan priest, a religious order priest, a deacon, a sister, a brother, a monk, and so on? Who actually receives the sacrament of Holy Orders?"

For starters, the sacrament of Holy Orders is that by which one becomes a bishop or priest. One becomes "another Christ," or "*in persona Christi*," which means "in the person of Christ." It's then, as another Christ, that the bishop or priest carries out his duties of teaching, guiding, sanctifying, and serving the people of God in accordance with the responsibilities to the office in which they were ordained. Deacons receive the sacrament of Holy Orders too, but unlike a priest or bishop, they are not ordained "*in persona Christi*," but are rather ordained to assist priests and bishops.

A sister, brother, monk, or priest of a religious order, such as the Carmelites, Benedictines, Franciscans, Dominicans, Jesuits, Trappists, and so on — live, pray, and work in community with each other and follow a way of life in accordance to the constitution or rule of their particular order, as established by the founder of that order. The ministry and work of these different communities can vary quite a bit. Some work in education, some in health care; some work with the poor and are involved in missionary work in foreign countries; others may be contemplative or monastic communities and focus solely on a life of prayer and self-sustaining work. Such a life is offered up as a perpetual prayer for the whole world, and we all are keenly aware of the need for lots of prayers for our world!

Those in religious orders are consecrated to the Lord and take vows of poverty, chastity, and obedience. The process of becoming a sister, brother, monk, or priest usually takes place in stages as the individual becomes more familiar with the life and mission of the order and becomes more ready to fully enter into that life. It is not something to rush into. Priests of religious orders follow the same way of life as others in their particular communities, but differ because they have also received the sacrament of Holy Orders, so they also take on priestly duties and responsibilities.

Deacons, having received the sacrament of Holy Orders, will fall into one of two categories: a permanent deacon or a transitional deacon. A transitional deacon is one who is "transitioning" into the priesthood. Toward the end of one's seminary training, an individual will first be ordained a deacon, serve in a parish for a year or so, and then if found ready and worthy, he will go on to priesthood ordination. A permanent deacon on the other hand, is one who will remain a deacon and not go on to the priesthood. A permanent deacon can be married and have a family as long as the marriage took place *before* ordination. If his wife should pass away at some point, he would then be eligible to go on to priesthood (with permission from his bishop).

A deacon assists the priest at Mass, can help (to varying degrees) with the administration of other sacraments and can perform the sacrament of Baptism by himself. Deacons are often involved in things like marriage and baptismal preparation, in educational activities such as the Rite of Christian Initiation for Adults, and with many of the same things that a parish priest is involved in. The work and ministry of a deacon will vary from place to place and depends on what the needs of the parish are or what the pastor or associate pastor needs help with. Some deacons work full time in a parish, some part time, still others help out on just the weekends. Many permanent deacons have a regular full-time job outside the Church, and some enter the deaconate after retirement. Again, there are various service opportunities for deacons.

A diocesan priest generally serves in the parishes of a particular diocese (or archdiocese). A diocese is a territory of parishes that the pope places under the care and leadership of a bishop or archbishop. An archdiocese is essentially the headquarters for a particular area. For example, Missouri is divided into four sections/dioceses, and St. Louis is the archdiocese.

A diocesan priest lives, serves, and leads a parish community. His primary role (as with all priests) is to administer the sacraments and preach the gospel. If this is not a priest's top priority, then he might as well go join the circus, because that's what his life will become. A parish priest is to be whole-heartedly devoted to bringing Christ to the people in the Eucharist, to exercise the mercy of Christ through the sacrament of Reconciliation, to bring new members into the Church and into God's family through Baptism. A priest is to bring the healing love of Jesus to those in need through the sacrament of Anointing of the Sick. He is to unite couples in Christ's love through Holy Matrimony. To foster and make available the sacramental life of the Church is why a priest becomes a priest, along with teaching, preaching, and living the Gospel, of course.

Accompanying his sacramental duties, a parish priest is involved (to varying degrees) with the administration of a parish. A diocesan priest plans (or at least should oversee) liturgical events, educational programs, retreats, and is involved in a multitude of parish activities and organizations. He will spend a good deal of time going to nursing homes and hospitals, visiting shut-ins, teaching in schools, sitting in on countless meetings to ensure that things in the parish are heading in the right direction. A

parish priest is with his people through all stages of life, from a
child's birth to the burial of a loved one. He is with his people in
the best of times, the worst of times, and everything in between.
His presence is a ministry in and of itself, and it should signify the
presence of Christ. And of course, lest one may forget, a priest
needs to pray, and pray like mad!

Diocesan priests make a promise of obedience to their bishop
(and his successors) and a promise of celibacy. They do not take
a vow of poverty, as many mistakenly believe. Diocesan priests
live and serve in the secular world. They earn a (meager) wage,
have to pay taxes, and with a few exceptions, have to provide for
themselves like anybody else. Although we don't live a life of
promised poverty, a diocesan priest should strive to live a life of
relative simplicity, as all Christians are called to do.

The promise of obedience that a priest takes does not mean
that he must jump off a bridge, dye his hair blue, or cut off his
right arm just because his bishop says so. The promise of obedience is to ensure that a priest is working with his bishop (not
against him) and is thus ultimately working with and for Christ
to serve the people of God and to be faithful to the teachings of
the Church as handed on from Jesus to the apostles. This of
course demands that the bishop is also faithful to his calling and
is himself in union with the pope, the teachings of Christ and the
Church, and is not using his authority and position to do whatever he wants and promote his own agenda.

CELIBACY ISSUES

THE PROMISE OF CELIBACY means that a priest will never marry.
This issue is a topic of great controversy and discussion in our
current time, as it has been for centuries. Raymond Arroyo, in an

article entitled "Celibacy: The Fact and Fiction,"[17] does an excellent job of clarifying things. He states,

> If you believe the folks on TV, celibacy was something "imposed on the priesthood" during the Middle Ages to keep the children of clerics from inheriting Church property. If I had a dime for every time I've heard this. . . . Actually, the real history is far more interesting, and complex. To begin with, Christ himself was a celibate so it is no surprise that the early Church and Scripture itself salutes and commends the practice. In Matthew's Gospel, Christ lauds those who "make themselves eunuchs for the sake of the kingdom of heaven." In his first letter to the Corinthians, St. Paul, another celibate writes: "the unmarried man is anxious about the affairs of the Lord . . . but the married man is anxious about worldly affairs, how to please his wife, and his interests are divided."

Arroyo goes on to point out that,

> From the time of Christ forward, celibacy was the Catholic norm for priests; married clergy were merely tolerated. Certainly by the 4th century there is little doubt where the Church stood on the matter. In 385, Pope Siricius issued the first papal decree on priestly celibacy. Five years later, the Council of Carthage announced: "Previous councils have decreed that bishops, priests, and deacons must be continent and perfectly chaste, as becomes ministers of God . . . as the Apostles taught." By the Council of Toledo in 633, a bishop's permission was needed for a priest to marry. Finally in 1139, Pope Gregory VII declared celibacy mandatory

for all priests; formalizing in law what was already the general practice for centuries.

So what about this notion that protecting Church land rights drove the papacy to the discipline of celibacy? Arroyo concludes,

> It just isn't true. But there is a spiritual explanation. Starting in the third century married priests were required to abstain from sex the night before offering Mass. The notion being: Separate yourselves from the worldly and focus on the transcendent. As the demand for the sacraments increased, these men were abstaining from sex all the time. Thus, like all things in the Church, a practice rooted in tradition evolved over time and eventually was codified into law.

There are also more practical reasons for celibacy. Besides abstaining from marriage as an imitation of Christ's ministry and as a way of making a sacrifice of one's flesh (as Christ made a sacrifice of his flesh on the cross), celibacy is also a way of life, a gift that enables the priest to dedicate his entire being to his people and the Church as a whole. For a priest, his parishioners and the people he serves *are* his family. A priest is literally married to the Church. For a priest to have two families and two brides would be chaotic. And this is evident in the fact that amongst protestant ministers, the divorce rate is quite high. Believe it or not, celibacy is actually something that many protestant ministers feel they would benefit greatly from.

Something else that many are not aware of is that there are in fact some married Roman Catholic priests. There are some instances where a minister of another Christian denomination, who is married and has a family, has gained permission to become a Roman Catholic priest. These men are the first to give witness as to how extremely difficult (and often unfair) it is to be the "father" of two different families.

Many critics say, "Celibacy is just not natural." And they are right, it isn't natural, it is a supernatural way of life. It can only be lived with the grace of God, and it is thus a powerful sign to the people of God that the Lord can and will give us the grace, courage, and strength to deal with any cross that we must carry or any thing life may bring before us.

As any priest or religious brother or sister can attest to, it's truly amazing the things that the Lord does through our ministry. It's very humbling. We are well aware of our countless weaknesses and shortcomings, and we are the first to recognize that if anything good and significantly fruitful happens through us, it is truly the work of the Lord. God chooses the weak and lowly to be his instruments. I'm the first to admit that if anything good comes out of my mouth or out of my head, or if I do anything that is of real value and purpose for the people of God, then you (and I) can be sure that it is God using me and working through me for that purpose, because let me tell you, I'm a big dumb foolish idiot! (Well, maybe I'm not that big and dumb and foolish, but you get the point.)

Another issue that comes up rather frequently these days concerning celibacy is its effect and possible role in the clergy sex-abuse crisis. Many say, "If these priests were allowed to get married, they would not be so sexually frustrated and would not be abusing people, especially the youth." The reality is that this is just not true. If celibacy led to sexual abuse, then the millions of single men and women out there who by choice are not currently sexually active would all be on the top of the suspect list as potential abusers, and this of course would be ridiculous! First of all, as I pointed out earlier, the vast majority of priests and religious are not molesting kids and sexually abusing people at all.

The greatest numbers of people who have sexually abused others or who are full-blown sexual predators are not celibate clergymen. Most of them are individuals who are married or who are single, sexually active people, not celibates. Such abusers come from all walks of life, and all social statuses. Being allowed to have a wife and a family, or even on a more basic level, the ability to be sexually active, does not cure the sickness that is at the root of sexual abuse. For the priests who have committed these horrible crimes, it is their *failure* to properly live out their call to celibacy that has opened the door for their sickness to take over.

WOMEN'S ORDINATION?

ANOTHER ISSUE THAT celibacy takes the blame for is the lack of vocations to the priesthood and religious life. Here again, celibacy is not to blame. Other denominations that allow their priests or ministers to be married are hurting for numbers just as bad as we, and some even worse. Another proposed solution to the priest shortage that comes up quite frequently is to ordain women. Entire movements have been started in response to this subject, and it has sparked many violent debates across the land, so I'll just get right to the point. The bottom line concerning women's ordination is that the Church simply does not have the authority to do so. It's not a matter of not wanting to, it is not a matter of being sexist, and it is certainly not a matter of women being unable to do the job. The fact of the matter is that the Church sincerely can't do it. No one in the Church and no one on earth (including the pope) has the authority to change the precedent that Jesus himself set forth.

As we know from Scripture, Jesus had many followers, both men and women, and we also know that Jesus (for whatever reason) specifically chose twelve men for a specific mission. He gave those twelve distinct authority and responsibility. Jesus was certainly not a "male chauvinist pig," and even though it was without question a male-dominated society at the time, Jesus always made it a point to treat women with great respect and dignity. Maybe Jesus chose men (you'll like this ladies . . . sorry guys) because we are so irresponsible, unfaithful, and foolish at times.

We see in Scripture how Jesus' twelve disciples constantly failed him, how they denied him, how they abandoned him when he needed them most. Who was it that stuck by Jesus' side at the crucifixion? Mostly women. Who was it that Jesus first appeared to, and who actually believed and had faith that he had risen from the dead? Again, women. Perhaps the Lord knew that we men do so many stupid things that if anything good happens through us, it is a sure sign of the power and presence of God. So again, the bottom line is that for whatever reason, Jesus specifically chose twelve men, and the Church simply does not have the authority to deviate from this directive. We cannot rewrite the gospels to suit our likes and dislikes. Priesthood is not a right, it is a calling. One does not choose to become a priest, one is chosen.

Another theological reality that comes into play here, as I pointed out a moment ago, is that a priest is ordained to be "another Christ." We know from Scripture that Jesus referred to himself as the "bridegroom" and his Church as the "bride." There was and is a real, authentic spousal relationship. This is why the Church is always referred to as "she." So, priests are literally married to the Church. The Church is our bride. Our promise of celibacy enables us to be spiritually fertile, to bring about many spiritual children to God's family and to enable us to be a good "father" to them. In the eyes of God, a marriage is only between a man and a woman. Thus, a woman as priest would completely contradict this divinely instituted framework. Women can't become priests for the same reason men can't give birth to children:

it simply is not the way God had planned, and all the fussing in the world won't change it.

VOCATIONAL DISCERNMENT

WITH OUR TERMS DEFINED now and perhaps a little better understanding of some of the issues that concern religious vocations, the next question is, "How does one know whether he or she is being called to religious life?" Answering that question is what we call the process of discernment. To discern a vocation (any vocation for that matter) is a process of asking, and then carefully, with brutal honesty, answering those important questions of: What do I want to do with my life? What is most important to me? How can I best love and serve God? What gifts do I have? What weaknesses do I have? What makes me feel most alive? What brings me peace and satisfaction? What do I truly feel called to in life? And so on.

Such questions as these need careful, thoughtful, and precise consideration. They are not things to rush through and come up with the first answer that pops into one's head like an ill-fated effort at passing a history test that one did not adequately study for. They are things to mull over and reflect upon with great diligence and patience. Most importantly, they are things to bring to prayer.

Some things to keep in mind while discerning are, first of all, even though God may be calling one to a particular vocation, one still has the choice to say, "No." And God will not hate your guts and send you straight to hell if this is your answer. God loves us and respects our decisions, even if they make us miserable. God will not force us to do anything in life. But he does invite us to certain things, he does call us to certain things, and he knows that if we answer yes, that we can be extraordinary instruments for his love, grace, and presence in our world. God knows what we are best suited for and what we would be most happy and satisfied with in life, and he gently calls us in the direction of those things, but again, we can say no, and he will love us just the same.

One needs to keep in mind also that no matter what vocation one is called to and chooses in life, you can be darn good and sure that there will be a multitude of sacrifices to be made, that there will be much heartache, that one will experience suffering, pain, aggravations, obstacles, highs, lows, many victories, many defeats, and much turmoil and testing throughout your journey. No one gets a free ride and no matter what we choose as a vocation, we will still be living it out here on planet Earth with all its destruction, sin and evil.

A religious vocation is not a free pass to heaven or an exemption from the struggles that all humanity has to deal with. If one enters the priesthood or religious life as an attempt to escape personal defects, struggles, sinfulness, or fears of any kind, one will only be fooling him or herself and ultimately making his or her life (and possibly the lives of others) a living nightmare. No matter what God calls us to, he wants us to be holy, happy, and healthy in that vocation.

Something I constantly tell people regarding the priesthood is that there are many things I could have done with my life. There are things I might actually be better at, and possibly enjoy more at times, than being a priest. But when it's all said and done, there is nothing that I feel more called to do and more at peace with than being a priest. I know without a shadow of a doubt that this is where God has called me to be, and this is how I can best serve and love him and others.

MY VOCATION STORY

As I STATED IN THE OPENING of this chapter, many people ask us priests how we decided to become priests. Folks are very interested in our "vocation story." Well, I might as well tell you mine while I'm on the subject here.

I thought about becoming a priest at a very young age, probably in the second or third grade. I grew up in a large parish, and our church, St. Charles Borromeo, was (and still is) a big, beautiful, historic, magnificent building. It's an "old school" church with a huge, dramatic crucifix hanging in the front of the sanctuary and an enormous bank vault-like tabernacle that makes a loud, commanding noise when the doors open and shut, like the veil of reality cracking open to expose the glory of God! There are life-size statues of Mary and St. Joseph, as well as large, realistic Stations of the Cross. It has a sky-high ceiling with tall pillars and a long aisle. Sound reverberates off the granite walls with a grand luster. Light gently cascades down onto the faithful from the towering stained glass windows that bear witness to the talented craftsmen of decades ago. The two steeples reach high to the heavens, longing to touch the very face of God and whisper prayers into his timeless, omnipotent ear. My home parish is how a Catholic church should look, in my opinion. It truly gives the feel of a sacred place and elevates one's thoughts to the magnificence of God.

As with most young kids, I didn't quite get what was going on at church all the time, and as a result I found it to be boring more often than not. But still, being in that building affected me. It had a compelling, divinely inspired influence on me. I knew it was the house of God. Growing up in St. Charles Borromeo parish and receiving my initial education at the parish school, I witnessed the example of several fine priests, and unfortunately, I also witnessed the example of a few not-so-fine ones.

My pastor at the time was Msgr. Michael Owens. Msgr. Owens was an older man who was the pastor there for the better part of fifty years if I'm not mistaken. He was a tall, well-built, proud Irishman, who also happened to have been a chaplain during World War II.

Msgr. Owens had a very intimidating presence. He always had a deadly serious look on his face, and he moved slowly, but with great prominence and forethought. Every step he took would produce a loud, solid "clack" as his hard-soled shoes hit the pavement with notable distinction. He truly put the fear of God into us kids! He always seemed to be deep in thought. When he spoke, a thundering, authoritative voice would burst forth from somewhere way down deep in that towering figure of a man. Of course, the fact that he always wore his black cassock didn't soften his character any. To us kids, he was Darth Vader as a priest!

When he preached, he didn't need a microphone. That booming voice would shatter the silence of the stillness of church and echo through the air like a jet fighter piercing through the quiet, sunlit sky with deafening volume. He spoke with passionate conviction and unquestionable supremacy. He told us stories, anecdotes, and personal experiences that often shook us to the core and really made us think. I can vividly recall many of them still today. And if some wise-cracking, punk, eighth graders joked around during Mass, he'd stop and let them have it right there in front of God and everybody. You didn't mess with Msgr. Owens! If a student got in big trouble at school, he or she begged, pleaded, and prayed to be sent to the principal's office instead of having to go see Monsignor.

In more recent years, I've found out through some of his brother priests who are still alive and kicking, that Msgr. Owens' nickname was "Iron Mike." But despite his iron-clad, no-nonsense approach to things, it was obvious that he loved and cared for all of us very much. And he did have a sense of humor; it was just hard to see at times, except on St. Patrick's Day, when he would sing Irish songs, tell jokes, wear all kinds of crazy outfits, and actually let us off school early. Monsignor was so very passionate and hard-edged about certain things, because he knew well the challenges we would be facing as we grew into adults. He armed us well for the possibilities of life's hardships and temptations with his words and with the grace of the sacraments. After all, as a military chaplain, he was a man who was willing to take a bullet for the people of God!

It was serving Mass for Msgr. Owens that first opened my ears and eyes to the vocation of the priesthood. I can vividly recall kneeling down at the side of the altar watching him say the Eucharistic prayer. As he gazed into the host and said the words, "This is my body . . . ," his eyes lit up with an other-worldly glow. When he took the chalice in his strong hands and said, "This is my blood . . . ," it was as if he was looking into the very eyes of Jesus Christ, and really, he was. He said Mass with such conviction and passion that it just blew me away. I knew that something profoundly sacred was taking pace, and that is what I wanted to be a part of and do myself one day.

Something else about Msgr. Owens that has always stuck with me was his prayerfulness. Over the years I've heard many who knew Monsignor recall how difficult he was to work with or how overbearing he could often be. Some have been quick to point out his weaknesses and the things he struggled with, but I can honestly say that he is the only priest I have *ever* met, besides Pope John Paul II, who before *every* Mass he ever said, was down on his knees, totally immersed in intense prayer. He took his sacramental duties, and especially the celebration of Mass, deadly seriously, as they should be taken. He never said anything to me about becoming a priest, although he often encouraged vocations. I really didn't personally know him at all, but it was simply my exposure to his presence and his priestly passion that made me want to become a priest myself, and it is his example that continues to inspire me today.

As I got older, that desire to become a priest began to fade. By the time I was in eighth grade or so and then going on to high school, becoming a priest was the last thing on my mind. I didn't like going to church at all, and I only went because my parents made me (thanks, Mom and Dad). At that time in my life, I was busy trying to be the world's greatest rock-and-roll guitar player, trying to break the high school bench press record, and doing a lot of stupid things and getting myself into a fair amount of trouble.

Like many young people, I began to question everything in life and to disagree with what (I thought) was the Church's stance on things. I was rebellious, distant, surly, and had a very negative outlook on life in general. I had no idea what I wanted to do with my life and what the future held for me. I didn't have any long-term aspirations, and frankly, I really didn't care about much of anything. I didn't spend Friday and Saturday nights at high school football games cheering on Frankie Quarterback. I instead worked on the weekends at lousy restaurants with drug-pushing losers, promiscuous teenage vixens, and militant, homosexual college theater students. It was a real reality check and an education all in itself. I was exposed to people and things that, until then, I'd only seen on sensational daytime talk shows.

I thankfully never got totally sucked into the heavy-duty drug scene that I was constantly around, but I'll admit that I did tend to overindulge on alcohol with my friends on the weekends to drown my miserable existence. High school for me is still a blur today. It was such a miserable, depressing time that I simply seemed to have erased those memories.

When I went on to college, I had cleaned up my act quite a bit, thankfully, but still had no idea what to do with my life. I figured, "Well, my brother majored in music, I'm a good guitar player, and I love music, so I guess I'll major in music as well." And so I went on to major in music as a classical guitarist.

It was during those first couple of years of college that I had a conversion back to the faith and the Church. In the fallout of the destructive way of life I'd been living, I began to realize the emptiness and pointlessness of it all. One evening I officially invited God back into my life and began to pray. Those daily prayer sessions got longer and longer, and by the end of the year I was spending several hours in prayer every day. It was that renewed relationship with the Lord that then spurred me on to explore the Catholic faith for myself, to truly take ownership of it — which I was supposed to do at Confirmation.

I began to re-educate myself about what we believe and why we profess to believe it. I wrestled with those tough questions and intellectually put myself through the ringer. I was consumed with the search for truth, and whether or not the Catholic Church genuinely contained the fullness of that truth. I spent countless, sleepless nights pondering issues of faith. I bombarded myself with all those "What if . . . ?" questions. I plunged myself mercilessly into an interior, spiritual odyssey.

When I look back at those reconversion experiences, I see it now as if the Holy Spirit was purifying me and preparing me to answer the biggest question of all: "Am I being called to the priesthood?" And the result of all that prayer and spiritual exercising was, in fact, a renewed call to the priesthood. When I would actually think about myself as a priest, I could definitely see it as possibility; it seemed right. But at the same time, I tried to put the idea out of my head. I wanted to get married and have a family. I still had no clue what I was going to do with my life and what kind of career or work I would eventually end up in, but I could certainly see myself married and having kids.

Thus began that discernment process of prayerfully asking all those hard questions and answering them with brutal honesty. During that process I felt the call to priesthood get stronger and stronger, and as it did, I tried to deny it more and more. I even went back to some of my old ways to prove to God that I'm too much of a sinner and not worthy to be a priest. Of course, I didn't realize at that time that nobody is ever worthy of it, it is he who calls and chooses us with all our imperfections and weakness.

Thinking back to those days, I can vividly recall sitting around at a college party (and I'm going to be honest here), being half-liquored up with a girl I didn't even know hanging all over me, and in the midst of that still having this overwhelming feeling of being called to the priesthood. Now don't get me wrong, it's not that I didn't like lovely ladies hanging all over me, but I simply knew that I was being called to something else.

As time went on, that call got so strong that I simply could not run or hide anymore. The "Hound of Heaven" got me! I finally said, "All right, God. You win. I'll check out this priesthood stuff." And so I visited with the vocation director for the archdiocese, got some information on the seminary, and went to an introductory meeting. Even though I was still a bit apprehensive, I decided to take the plunge. After going through all the physical, psychological, and academic testing that prospective students must go through these days (which is a very good thing), I was accepted and officially became a seminarian.

The summer before my first year of seminary started, I figured I had better really get my act together. That summer was the holiest I had ever been in my life up to that point! I went to daily Mass; prayed non-stop; did tons of spiritual reading; gave a good portion of my summer earnings to charitable causes; didn't drink at all; didn't cuss, spit, or even listen to my beloved rock-and-roll music. That summer I had the mellow sounds of Gregorian chant blasting out my window as I hauled down the highway. I must admit that I just didn't feel like myself. I felt like I was stuffing myself into a suit that just didn't fit. But I carried on.

Finally, the first day of seminary came, and as I moved my things into a tiny cell-like room, which would be my home for the next several years, the reality that it was going to be a loooooooooong eight years hit me like a ton of bricks. (It actually went by fast as lightning!) During that first week, I was in for one shock after the next. I couldn't believe it! People were not walking around in a stoic silence. They were not decked out in long robes and solemnly chanting as they roamed about the seminary grounds. There were guys playing basketball and shooting pool. They were listening to Van Halen on the radio, and I regularly heard loud, jovial laughter. "What is wrong with these guys?" I kept asking myself. The seminary was not supposed to be like this . . . filled with normal guys doing normal things. What was going on here!?

After that initial shock wore off, I soon realized, and was pleasantly surprised, that this was not a place of medieval rigor filled with religious fanatics. There were a few odd characters, I must admit, as there are in every walk of life, but I found that, for the most part, these guys and this place were good, healthy, and challenging, and it was fun to be there.

It was also a holy place. When it came time to pray together or celebrate Mass, those things were carried out with the utmost reverence and respect. It was then that I realized the truth of what Sr. Zoe (one of the seminary instructors . . . may she rest in peace) told me the first day there. She said, "Jesus calls all different kinds of men to be priests. You all have different talents, interests, personalities, and gifts. And God will use those differences to reach different people in different ways." I knew then it was okay to be me. I didn't have to "stuff myself into a suit that just didn't fit." God wanted me to be a priest and yet still be the person that he made me, while of course striving for virtue and holiness.

With that realization firmly in place, I went through the rest of my seminary years and eventually into the priesthood while still being true to God and also to myself. As another now-deceased priest told me, "Be your own man, be a good and holy man, and then be that man for God and his people." There was, and still is, great peace, comfort, and reassurance in doing so.

As time went on, I took a year off in the middle of my seminary education to re-evaluate things and catch my breath from all the schoolwork. During that year I began to have vocational doubts once again and thought that maybe I should just move on to something else. But all that changed when I befriended a priest who was sent to my parish by the name of Fr. Xavier Albert. Fr. Albert's passion and zeal for the Lord, which especially came shining through when he said Mass, affected me just as much as serving Mass as a boy for Msgr. Owens did. Being present when Fr. Albert was at the altar reminded me, without a doubt, that I too belong there at the altar as a priest.

That year, during the Mass on Easter Sunday, as Fr. Albert raised the host in the air at the consecration, an indescribable peace filled my soul, something came over me that immediately wiped away all apprehensions and fears. I simply knew it was time to go back to the seminary and continue plowing onward.

All in all, my seminary years were the greatest, yet most challenging years of my life. I wouldn't change them for anything. Reflecting back now, I see more clearly than ever how the Lord truly calls men and women from all walks and ways of life to serve him in religious vocations. The calling is often gentle, it's often faint, and yet at other times it's with skull-crushing volume. We hear in Scripture, "The harvest is plentiful, but the labors are few" (Lk 10:2). The Lord is calling many to his service, but many refuse to listen, and for others that calling is snatched away and snuffed out like a stinking, smoldering cigarette butt. As I mentioned earlier, the Lord does not force us to do anything in life. He simply says, "Follow me." Be assured that to do so will be difficult, it will not be an easy ride, but in answering, "Yes," to that call, one will experience the fullness of God's will — the peace, love, and satisfaction that no other way of life could ever bring.

CHAPTER 9

BE HEALED!

Close your eyes . . . better yet, tear them out. There is no more light to be seen. Take a step forward, six feet down. The tap on the shoulder is a point to the grave. Red roses are withered, their scent now sickening, a pungent reminder of the parlor to come. The stained glass is broken, replaced with bricks: wind beaten, blood-red, and cold. Illumination is forever snuffed out. Hope is snatched away while a worm from the earth is plucked. . . . see the ravens in flight. An atrophied smile and a crack-ribbed laugh, that's all that's left for now. Never again will teeth be exposed to broadcast cheer or reflect the sullen moon.

The sun rises, a new day dawns: the greatest pain of all. A blessing of life, yet no desire to live . . . the thieves have come again. The concrete cures and the heart becomes stone, the green has faded away. The reasons for joy? As many as the stars, but the heavens can't be seen while staring at the mud. A tired neck can raise a troubled brow no more. The wolves howl in the distant night, they'll come again to feed on souls. The shroud of black covers life once again. Its beauty unseen till the darkness of night is gone. But for now, just bleed.

EVERYBODY HAS A DISEASE

I WROTE THE PRECEDING, dismal, morbid poem one evening after reflecting on a conversation I had with a young man who was struggling greatly with depression. I was trying to empathetically work through the horrid mental and emotional anguish he was suffering to better get a grasp on his condition to try to be of some help, or at least to be better able to understand the nature of his suffering and torment.

On the outside, this young man was the epitome of health and youthful vigor. He had lots of friends, was fairly popular at school, had a girlfriend, was bright and intelligent, possessed great athletic ability, and seemed to have everything going for him. Yet, in the midst of it all, his life was a living hell. There was a rotting sorrow deep down in the core of his being that was eating him alive. It was as if he was in the nefarious, stertorous grip of an emotional malefactor that would not release him. He simply could not, and was truly incapable, of feeling or experiencing the joy of the good life he had. The eyes of his soul were cemented shut by the disease of depression.

His emotional pain seemed to be equally as intense as the physical pain of someone dying from bone cancer. The mental anguish he experienced and wrestled with daily was on par with the turmoil of someone suffering from diabetes. The gravity of his disability, the inability to perceive joy, was just as intense as the blind who cannot see the light of day or the deaf who cannot hear the voice of others.

The more that I, as a priest, witness the struggles in the lives of so many different people, and the more I walk along with them on the paths of their journey through life, the more I recognize an often unseen reality: everybody has a disease. When I use the word "disease" here, I'm referring to a sickness or a malady of various kinds, either mental/emotional, physical, spiritual, occupational, or environmental.

Very often, only those diseases of which we can see dramatic, outward manifestations move us to great pity for the individuals who are suffering from them, and rightly so. When we see a poor soul lying in a hospital bed with tubes entering and exiting every orifice of the body, whose flesh is bruised, dried, and crusted, whose breathing is forced with complicated machinery as he or she holds on to life by a thread, we are naturally inebriated with sympathy and compassion. We say to ourselves, "Good God . . . why does that person have to suffer so much? How horrible that must be!" But make no mistake about it, the intensity of that pain is, or will be eventually, present in all of us in one way or another. We all will have a disease, or diseases to suffer sooner or later — that's the unfortunate reality of life on earth.

SUFFERING AND SIN

KEEP IN MIND, it was no different for Jesus. As I've mentioned in some of my previous writing, Christ brought healing, peace, hope, the love of God, and ultimately salvation into the world, but he also experienced suffering, just like the rest of us. He, the Son of God, experienced betrayal, humiliation, and rejection — just like the rest of us. He, the Incarnate Word, experienced hunger, homelessness, imprisonment, torture, and death — just as we, too, will one day die. But, he, the Son of God, rose from the dead, and by means of his resurrection, we, too, are given the hope of resurrection and eternal life.

We obviously live in a wonderful world, in a world filled with incredible beauty. But nonetheless, our world is unfortunately dominated by sin. That first sin of Adam and Eve, that "original sin" of rejecting God, has poisoned everyone and everything in our world from then until now. Death, disease, personal tragedy, horrific acts of violence, and injustices are not punishments for sin, but they certainly can be the result of sin. AIDS is not a punishment for deviant and promiscuous sexual behavior and drug use, but it can be a result. Lung cancer and heart disease are not a punishment for abusive smoking, but they can be a result. Homelessness, hunger, poverty, war, all the things that plague our world — all have their roots somewhere, at some point in time, in sin, in that initial turning away from God. And unfortunately *all* of humanity suffers as a result of the sins of humanity.

We often hear about the need for social justice in our world and in our Church, but we forget and easily overlook the reality that, as Fulton Sheen once pointed out, "When we have individual justice, then we will have social justice!" Our individual sin, our personal sin, is that which leads to our social sin. If every human being on the face of the earth, if every baptized Christian, eradicated the sin from his or her life, our "social sin" would disappear. As our Lord said, "First take the log out of your own eye, and then you will see clearly to take the speck out of your brother's eye" (Mt 7:5).

Sin has a tremendous domino effect. One person's sin can cause a chain reaction that can negatively affect the lives of many innocent people, and sometimes that effect doesn't show up and manifest itself until many years down the road. We all love the ability to freely choose our own path, to freely make decisions for ourselves. We all love the free will that God has given us, and he has given us that freedom so that we may authentically love and be loved, but the flip side is that our choices and decisions, when made in disobedience to God's commands, can give birth to tremendous destruction: personal destruction (spiritually, physically, mentally) and eventually social destruction.

With all that being said, though, we still see innocent children dying from leukemia. We see perfectly healthy people suddenly being struck down with a terrible disease. We even saw a pope (John Paul II) suffer the crippling effects of Parkinson's disease. We see so many bad things happening to so many good people. What we often don't see or don't realize, however, is that just as many bad things happen to bad people. The reality is that bad things happen to *all* people.

The bottom line is that we live in an imperfect world. As an old philosophy instructor once pointed out, our world can produce someone as good and holy as Mother Teresa or someone as evil as Adolph Hitler. Our world can produce something as beautiful as a rainbow or something as destructive as a tornado. The bad things in our world are something we all experience. Some experience it to a greater degree, some to a lesser degree. For some it is a direct result of their own sinfulness, poor choices, or bad decisions, for others it's the result of someone else's sinfulness, poor choices, or bad decisions. And many of these poor choices and bad decisions are not originally made with ill intent. Who would have known thirty years ago that exposure to certain things would cause cancer? Who would have known that certain things in our diet and our environment that we took for granted could eventually do us much harm? Who would have known that building houses and subdivisions in a particular place would one day be in the direct path of a natural disaster?

Many theologians over the years have stated that Jesus did not come to remove suffering from the world. He — God, that is — instead came to enter into our suffering with us. He does not abandon us (though we often abandon him) even in those times when our suffering is a direct result of our own sinfulness. It is he who wishes to comfort us in our suffering. It is he who teaches us to take up our cross and to follow him. It is he who wishes to heal us of our disease as he did for so many when he walked the earth.

Whereas one's disease may be that of the darkness of depression, another's may be the enslavement and helpless addiction to one thing or another. Whereas one may experience the sickness of cancer, the other may be tortured by the inability to conceive a child. Whereas one may suffer the crippling effects of severe arthritis, another may grapple with the constant humiliation of unemployment. Whereas one clumsily hobbles along in constant discomfort with a prosthetic limb, another endures the brunt of an abusive parent or spouse. We all will be stricken, we all will suffer. We can run and hide, but there is no escape. There is, however, hope and an unlimited potential for good in the midst of our suffering.

REDEMPTIVE SUFFERING

St. Augustine once stated in his work *Enchiridion*, "Since God is the supreme good he would permit no evil in his works unless he were so omnipotent and good that he could produce good even out of evil." To that, St. Thomas Aquinas added, "This is part of the infinite goodness of God, that he should allow evil to exist, and out of it produce good." (*Summa Theologica* 1, 2, 3). So even though evil is not of God (it's the result of rejecting God), he still allows it so that good may result from it, but that is up to us.

As we've already seen, suffering is for the most part a result of sin and evil, ours or that of others. But at times, God gives us a cross of suffering to carry that does not have its origins in sin and evil. In the Gospel of John, we hear the story of Jesus and his disciples passing a man who had been born blind:

> And his disciples asked him, "Rabbi, who sinned, this man or his parents, that he was born blind?" Jesus answered, "It

was not that this man sinned, or his parents, but that the works of God might be made manifest in him" (Jn 9:2-3).

And then Jesus spat on the ground and made a clay of the spittle and anointed the man's eyes with the clay, healing the man's blindness.

No matter what the roots of our sufferings may be, when we find ourselves immersed in them, we can drown ourselves in self-pity, we can self-medicate with all kinds of things that only make matters worse, or we can carry the cross of suffering with dignity and with courage, and, most importantly, we can unite our sufferings to those of Christ.

Something we don't hear much about these days is "redemptive suffering." This is one of the most powerful forms of prayer on earth! Let me explain: Like many of you, I'm sure, a phrase I heard quite often as a youngster was, "Offer it up!" Whenever I complained about having to do my chores, eat stewed tomatoes, study for a test, or anything else I didn't want to do, my parents would say to me without delay, "Offer it up!" This was a phenomenon that I began to think was some kind of community conspiracy. At school, when I (dishonestly) told the teacher I had to go to the bathroom (just to get out of the monotony of math class for awhile), she'd say, "No, you'll have to wait till class is over, so offer it up!" Then at Church on Sunday, I'd hear it again from our priests, "Offer this up . . . offer that up!" I expected to hear that slogan from the president of the United States before it was all over!

As I got older I realized the power and implications of those words. In our prayers, and in our participation in the "priesthood of the faithful" (remember that from Chapter 3?), we are constantly offering things ("spiritual sacrifices") to God: usually our words and our time. When we take our offerings/sacrifices to the next level, when we offer God our talents, our treasure, our daily struggles as well as our joys and blessings, we put some serious meat on the bones of our sacrifices and offerings to God.

With the exception of the Eucharistic sacrifice at Mass, the preeminent offering that we can give to God, the most peerless sacrifice that we can offer him is our suffering, just as Jesus offered his passion and brutal death as the sacrifice for our atonement and salvation.

When we offer up real pain, real agony, genuine anguish, and truly nonfictional suffering and misery and consciously unite that with the pain, agony, anguish, suffering and misery of Christ on the cross, we participate in another aspect of Christ's mission and ministry: his role as victim. A victim, in this sense, refers to the victim of a sacrifice. As we looked at earlier, in the Jewish tradition, the victim of sacrifice was often an animal that would be killed and sacrificed to God in atonement for sin. And so, Jesus was the victim of the sacrifice on Calvary, he was/is the Lamb of sacrifice (the "Lamb of God" as we say) whose sacrifice has taken away the sin of the world.

By means of our prayers we can do incredible things for souls and for the sanctification of the world. When we back up our prayers with the sacrifice of real pain and suffering, we are delivering some serious, knockout blows to the work of Satan in our lives and in the lives of others. When we give our pain to Christ, he transforms it into ammunition to knock the hell out of the evil one (literally) who seeks to destroy all that is of God. When we "offer it up," we offer it to the Lord who "makes all things new" (see Rev 21:5). So, as a holy man once said, *"Don't waste your pain!"* Use it to fight the good fight! And, as a result of doing so, the actual bite of the suffering becomes greatly diminished, the anxiety of our struggles and misery evolve into a sense of peace, and no matter what the outcome of our personal suffering may be, we are healed on a much deeper level than the mere physical. We also then bring the healing of Christ to untold millions! This is redemptive suffering!

Suffering can also be beneficial in other ways. Sometimes it's only by means of suffering that we are finally forced to open our eyes to see the things we have been ignoring that desperately need to be addressed for our own good or that of our loved ones. Suffering at times is the only thing that forces us to shut up and open our distracted ears to the voice of God that we've been drowning out and covering up for way too long! Sometimes our suffering is the only thing that will teach us a much needed life changing lesson.

Suffering can also be very educational. It amplifies the true nature of ourselves, as our will to commit sin is weakened, and the mask of career, wealth, or social status is nullified. Suffering can teach appreciation, gratitude, humility, and wisdom. We see this in the case of the story of the "Prodigal Son," who only by means of his mistakes and suffering came back to his senses and realized how good he had it and how foolish he'd acted. His suffering (though self-inflicted) brought about healing and reconciliation: it brought him back to life!

Over the years, I've heard countless stories and personal witnesses from folks whose lives were transformed for the better by means of suffering. I recall a very successful doctor revealing how it was not until he was diagnosed with cancer, and forced to quit his practice, that he finally learned to be a father to his children and a husband to his wife and that he truly came to know and love God. In the end, he said his cancer was a tremendous blessing to him and he wouldn't have traded it for anything . . . as crazy as that sounds to the rest of us.

I remember a prominent musician telling about how his hearing trouble and subsequent departure from the rock-and-roll lifestyle was the best thing that ever happened to him. I can recollect an artist revealing how the emotional turmoil of her adolescence unlocked a creativity within her that she never knew existed that carried her to great success as an adult.

Another story I remember well is that of a mother whose child had Down syndrome. Although having a child with severe mental and/or physical illness is many a parent's worst nightmare, this woman related how her son has such a remarkable gift for evoking love and kindness in so many people. It was not a matter of people feeling sorry for her son, it was that he truly had a gentleness, a sincerity, and a presence about him that just seemed to make people better as a result of being around him. He reminded people of the simple beauty and sacredness of life. His perspective and response to things we take for granted is an inspiration for all who come in contact with him. Even though there are a multitude of extra challenges and hardships that come along with caring for a child with any kind of disability, this mother certainly did not see her son's condition as some kind of horrible curse that some others might. She saw her child as one of the most wonderful human beings on the face of the earth, and I would agree with her.

I could go on and on with stories of similar situations, but in all these cases, good came from suffering because it was allowed to and it was actively sought. If those same folks would have just thrown in the towel, given up all hope, belly flopped into an ocean of self-pity, and just gone down with the ship in the midst of their suffering, no good would have come from it. It would have only been amplified all the more. The one good thing that came from the mind of the German philosopher Friedrich Nietzsche was his statement, "That which does not kill me only makes me stronger." I'm a firm believer in that. But again, the strength and goodness that can result from suffering only come if one works with it instead of against it, and most importantly, if one works in unity with the sufferings of Christ and in cooperation with the grace of God.

Well, I suppose that's enough about suffering for the moment. After all, this chapter is supposed to be about healing. One final thought though: for the love of God (literally), don't go looking for suffering! It will find you sooner or later! Though offering up the hardships and struggles that come our way is of the most importance, and making sacrifices for God is of immense value, going out and purposely making your life a miserable wreck is not the idea! We are not masochists!

THE DESIRE FOR HEALING

IN THE MIDST OF OUR SUFFERING and sickness, even though it can be beneficial as we've seen, the reality is that we want to be healed. Nobody likes being strung out with pain, being beaten down with mental or physical anguish, or having one's life be completely (or evenly partially) disjointed as a result of an illness. And the more serious and severe an illness is, the more immediately one wants that healing to come about. For many people in our self-serving society, God is of little, if any, importance in their lives, until they, or a loved one, become seriously ill and they hear the grim reaper knocking on the door with his cold, boney knuckles. It's then, and often only then, that so many truly turn to God with sincerity and devotion.

When frantic desperation for a cure sets in, some go to extremes and seek out healing and medical or spiritual miracles from any and all possible sources, good or evil. If there is even the slightest chance it may work, some will travel to the ends of the earth and spend their life savings to seek what perhaps may be a very risky, unproven surgical procedure. Others will experiment with a cocktail of dubious and dangerous medicines, herbs, or supplements in hope for healing.

In the face of illness, there are those who will enlist all sorts of "spiritual" help, such as faith healers or even new age witchdoctors, who promise a cure. Catholics ask for the sacrament of Anointing of the Sick in times of need, and some supplement that sacramental grace with things like visiting Marian shrines, going on a pilgrimage, or guzzling holy water from Lourdes hoping for divine intervention and miracles. Some of this seems extreme, but who can blame them? When someone we love is in misery, we naturally want to do anything possible, no matter how seemingly limited, bizarre, or risky to help. Desperate times lead one to desperate measures.

Concerning the sacrament of Anointing of the Sick, and all the sacraments for that matter, it is important to keep in mind what you've heard me say many times now: they are not magic, and they're not supposed to be. In the same way, Jesus' ministry was not one of magic. In Scripture we hear how Jesus became aggravated with those who constantly asked and looked for signs instead of hearing his words and having faith. Although Jesus healed and cured many people, there were still many that he did not. This was not the purpose for which he came. Jesus was not a divine social worker. In the gospels, when Jesus healed, there was always an underlying, more important reason for it. Jesus' healings were signs pointing to the coming of the Kingdom of God; they were manifestations of God's forgiveness, challenges and rewards for faith, and a way in which the reality of God entered into the lives of those who were sick and suffering. Jesus' healings were a foreshadowing of the ultimate healing that he came to give us: the healing from sin and death.

GOD AND HEALING

IT IS QUITE OBVIOUS that God does not always heal our bodily sickness when, where, and how we wish, and that reality will remain unchanged no matter how many checks one may send to a televangelist faith healer. The bottom line is that a cure or a healing is ultimately conditional upon the will of God. As mentioned earlier, although sickness and suffering were not an original part of God's plan, he allows it so that good may come from it, even though that good is sometimes very hard for us to see or comprehend.

Though faith and openness to God's will is of the utmost importance, when one is ill and undergoing suffering, one must also not neglect the practical remedies available. Even in Scripture we hear things such as St. Paul giving the medical advice, "No longer drink only water, but use a little wine for the sake of your stomach and your frequent ailments" (1 Tim. 5:23).

It is quite clear that God has blessed humanity with a potentially stunning intellect which is capable of producing miracles in its own right. Keep in mind the actuality of God working in and through humanity. After all, we are made in his image and likeness. God has blessed us with the ability to use (not abuse) and develop things (while mindful of proper stewardship) in his creation to sustain life, to comfort while in pain, to heal sickness, and cure disease.

The answer to our prayers of physical healing are often found in the medicine that people have developed through the inspiration of God, but we are sometimes too proud to take it, or worse yet, we can't afford it due to monopolizing, greedy pharmaceutical companies. The answer to our prayers for a cure might very well rest in the hands of a surgeon whom God has gifted with amazing skill, but whose help we can't acquire due to a lousy health insurance plan. Here again, personal sin leads to social sin, which makes many innocent people suffer. But of course, God is the one who usually gets the blame instead.

THE SACRAMENT OF ANOINTING OF THE SICK

THOUGH TECHNICALLY, GOD very well could miraculously cure every sick and suffering person on earth, he does not. As we explored in the beginning of this chapter, often time it's (unfortunately) only through our suffering that we are finally brought to true conversion of heart, that we learn some much needed life lessons, that we get a loud and clear wake-up call, and that we once and for all learn to implement some discipline in our lives. As I also pointed out earlier, our Lord did not necessarily come to take away our suffering, but to enter into it with us, to support us, strengthen us, and be present to us by means of his healing grace, and that is exactly what he does by means of the sacrament of Anointing of the Sick.

To better understand the institution and practice of this great sacrament, let's start by looking at Scripture. In Matthew 10:8, our Lord instructs His disciples to, "Heal the sick, raise the dead, cleanse lepers, cast out demons." Earlier in Matthew, we hear that Jesus was to fulfill what the prophet Isaiah spoke, "He took our infirmities and bore our diseases" (Mt 8:17). In Luke 9:2, we hear, "And he sent them out to preach the kingdom of God and to heal." Yet again, in Mark 6:13, we read, "They cast out many demons, and anointed with oil many that were sick and healed them." We hear over and over Jesus' directives to heal the sick and to lay hands on those who are ill.

Later, in the Acts of the Apostles, we see many accounts of this work of healing continuing just as our Lord had taught. Along the same lines, St. Paul, in his epistles, speaks of illness and healing, as do the letters of St. John and St. Peter. But St. James gives us the most detailed account of the actual administering of the sacrament of healing. In James 5:14–15, he writes, "Is any among you sick? Let him call for the elders of the Church, and let them pray over him, anointing him with oil in the name of the Lord; and the prayer of faith will save the sick man, and the Lord will raise him up; and if he has committed sins, he will be forgiven."

The *Catechism of the Catholic Church* expounds beautifully on these passages and also that of Sacred Tradition to give us a more detailed understanding. The Church teaches:

> "By the sacred anointing of the sick and the prayer of the priests, the whole Church commends those who are ill to the suffering and glorified Lord, that he may raise them up and save them. And indeed she [the Church] exhorts them to contribute to the good of the People of God by freely uniting themselves to the Passion and death of Christ." (CCC 1499)

The *Catechism* further explains:

> The Holy Spirit gives to some a special charism of healing so as to make manifest the power of the grace of the risen Lord. But even the most intense prayers do not always obtain the healing of all illnesses. (CCC 1508)

In such cases, we can learn from St. Paul, as the *Catechism* goes on to point out:

> Thus St. Paul must learn from the Lord that "my grace is sufficient for you, for my power is made perfect in weakness," and that the sufferings to be endured can mean that, "in my flesh I complete what is lacking in Christ's afflictions for the sake of his Body, that is, the Church." (CCC 1508)

With all this as the background, let's take a look at the nuts and bolts of the actual sacrament now. For starters, the Church states:

> The sacrament of Anointing of the Sick is given to those who are seriously ill by anointing them on the forehead and hands with duly blessed oil — pressed from olives or from other plants — saying, only once: "Through this holy anointing may the Lord in his love and mercy help you with the grace of the Holy Spirit. May the Lord who frees you from sin save you and raise you up." (CCC 1513)

Something to keep in mind here is that the term "seriously ill" has a few different connotations. For one, it refers to mental and spiritual illness along with the obvious physical illness. It also includes those who struggle with advanced age and those about to undergo surgery or treatment. It's also important to realize that the sacrament can be administered to one of any age, and it can be received more than once, given one has sufficient reason. One final distinction is that the sacrament of Anointing of the Sick is not "Last Rites," as it's often mistakenly called . . . more about that in a moment.

As with all the other sacraments, Anointing of the Sick is both a liturgical and a communal celebration. Given the nature of the sacrament, it can be (and most often is) administered in settings outside a Church, such as a home or hospital, but it is still most fitting for it to take place within the celebration of the Eucharist, or within the context of a penance or "healing" prayer service. A communal, liturgical celebration of the sacrament should include the following elements and actions to properly signify the grace the sacrament confers: Liturgy of the Word (use of Scripture), an act of repentance, the laying on of hands by a priest (who is the only one who can administer this sacrament), prayers said over the sick, and the actual anointing with blessed oil.

In regard to the "prayers" that are said as part of the sacrament, there are lots of different options. The *Rites of Anointing and Viaticum* (the official book we use to administer the sacrament properly) is loaded with different prayers for different situations and different settings that people may be in.

So what happens then? Does the sick person leap up out of bed with an instantaneous cure? Do the crippled walk, the blind see, the deaf hear, and the mute speak? Usually not, but there have been occasions of that happening. It's a little something we call miracles, and they do still happen. The *Catechism* explains with great detail what happens as a result of this sacrament. First of all:

> The first grace of this sacrament is one of strengthening, peace and courage to overcome the difficulties that go with the condition of serious illness or the frailty of old age. This grace is a gift of the Holy Spirit, who renews trust and faith in God and strengthens against the temptations of the evil one, the temptation to discouragement and anguish in the face of death. This assistance from the Lord by the power of his Spirit is meant to lead the sick person to healing of the soul, but also of the body if such is God's will. Furthermore, "if he has committed sins, he will be forgiven." (CCC 1520)

Secondly, there is the union with the passion of Christ. Remember — "redemptive suffering"? The Church explains it like this:

> By the grace of this sacrament the sick person receives the strength and the gift of uniting himself more closely to Christ's Passion: in a certain way he is consecrated to bear fruit by configuration to the Savior's redemptive Passion.

> Suffering, a consequence of original sin, acquires a new meaning; it becomes a participation in the saving work of Jesus. (CCC 1521)

As we've already seen, suffering can be of great value.

Thirdly, the recipient of the sacrament receives an ecclesial grace:

> The sick who receive this sacrament, "by freely uniting themselves to the passion and death of Christ," "contribute to the good of the People of God." By celebrating this sacrament, the Church, in the communion of saints, intercedes for the benefit of the sick person, and he, for his part, through the grace of this sacrament, contributes to the sanctification of the Church and to the good of all for whom the Church suffers and offers herself through Christ to God the Father. (CCC 1522)

Finally, the person who is anointed gains "a preparation for the final journey." The *Catechism* explains:

> If the sacrament of anointing of the sick is given to all who suffer from serious illness and infirmity, even more rightly is it given to those at the point of departing this life; so it is also called *sacramentum exeuntium* (the sacrament of those departing). The Anointing of the Sick completes our conformity to the death and Resurrection of Christ, just as Baptism began it. It completes the holy anointings that mark the whole Christian life: that of Baptism which sealed the new life in us, and that of Confirmation which strengthened us for the combat of this life. This last anointing fortifies the end

of our earthly life like a solid rampart for the final struggles before entering the Father's house. (CCC 1523)

And so, even though the sick or suffering person does not always attain an instant physical cure, he or she does experience the reality of Christ's healing, comfort, peace, strengthening, mercy, forgiveness, and love. By means of this sacrament, Christ truly enters into the infirm person's life and into their pain. As I've mentioned a few times already (once more can't hurt), Jesus did not necessarily come to take away our suffering, he came to enter into it with us, to help us to transform the bad into good, and most importantly to bring about redemption which we can participate in greatly by uniting our suffering to his.

VIATICUM

ALONG WITH THE SACRAMENT of Anointing of the Sick, the Church also makes available to those near death a rite called viaticum, which means, "food for the journey." Viaticum is the reception of Communion (after the opportunity for the sacrament of Reconciliation) for the last time. In this final reception of the sacraments (referred to by many as "the Last Rites"), the soul is nourished, cleansed, and strengthened with the grace of God and Christ himself in the Eucharist, as the person prepares to pass from this life to the next. It is here that the sacraments become a doorway from earth to eternity; they send the soul home to God. Of course the final judgment of that person is up to our Lord, but by means of the sacraments, and a truly contrite heart, they are healed.

WRAP-UP

WELL, THAT ABOUT WRAPS things up. It seems we've come to the end of the book. I don't really have any long summaries or closing reflections to add at this point because there is more on the way in a follow-up to *Meat & Potatoes Catholicism*. So, in the meantime, let all the information in this book digest well, and get ready to come back for another helping.

God bless you,
Fr. Joe Classen

ENDNOTES

CHAPTER 3. COME TO THE WATER

[1] International Committee on English in the Liturgy (ICEL), *Rite of Baptism for Children*, paragraph 91.

[2] ICEL, *Rite of Baptism for Children*, paragraph 76.

[3] ICEL, *Rite of Baptism for Children*, paragraph 76.

[4] ICEL, *Rite of Baptism for Children*, paragraph 77.

[5] ICEL, *Rite of Baptism for Children*, paragraph 78.

[6] ICEL, *Rite of Baptism for Children*, paragraph 88.

[7] ICEL, *Rite of Baptism for Children*, paragraph 93.

[8] ICEL, *Rite of Baptism for Children*, paragraph 98.

[9] ICEL, *Rite of Baptism for Children*, paragraph 99.

[10] ICEL, *Rite of Baptism for Children*, paragraph 99.

[11] ICEL, *Rite of Baptism for Children*, paragraph 100.

[12] ICEL, *Rite of Baptism for Children*, paragraph 103.

CHAPTER 6. FIRE AND FRUIT

[13] ICEL, *Rite of Confirmation (Second Edition)*, paragraph 25.

[14] ICEL, *Rite of Confirmation (Second Edition)*, paragraph 27.

CHAPTER 7. WEDDING BELLS TOLL

[15] This information is from "Cohabitation: The Marriage Enemy," by David Popenoe, and from the Pastoral Letter issued by the Kansas Bishops directed to engaged couples who cohabit and those involved in their marriage preparation. David Popenoe is professor of sociology and,

with Barbara Dafoe Whitehead, co-director of the National Marriage Project at Rutgers University, New Brunswick, N.J.

[16] Glenn T. Stanton is the Senior Research Analyst for Marriage and Sexuality at Focus on the Family, as well as the author of *Why Marriage Matters: Reasons to Believe in Marriage in Postmodern Society*.

CHAPTER 8. THE CALL

[17] Raymond Arroyo, "Celibacy: The Fact and the Fiction," *National Review*, May 16, 2002.